DEEP
REFLECTIONS

DEEP
REFLECTIONS

The Untold Truth

Book 1

by

SAYED AMIR HUSSAIN

Deep Reflections: The Untold Truth

© 2025 Sayed Amir Hussain

All rights reserved.

No part of this book may be reproduced, stored in a retrieval system, or transmitted in any form or by any means—electronic, mechanical, photocopying, recording, or otherwise—without prior written permission from the publisher, except for brief quotations used in reviews, criticism, or scholarly works.

First Edition: 2025

Published by UmmTaha Publications
Houston, Texas, USA
www.ummtaha.com

Printed in the United States of America
ISBN: 979-8-9939909-0-3

To my parents,

whose faith and guidance have been
the light of every reflection.
And to all who
strive to reflect,
to question, and
to rediscover truth.

AUTHOR'S NOTE

This work has emerged from a long, uneven journey —crafted in moments of strength and stretches of exhaustion, through days of clear words and days when writing felt impossible. It did not come from comfort. It slowly took shape, molded by memories that surfaced unexpectedly and by persistent questions.

What you will find here is not a polished narrative, but an honest one. The experiences of leadership, service, conflict, and quiet perseverance are recounted with all their complexity. Some have a raw, unfiltered edge; many continue to teach me the true demands of integrity. I've learned to focus less on constructing neat stories and more on recognizing grace in a journey of lessons still unfolding.

My aim has been neither to embellish nor to hide. My purpose is simple: to write truthfully, understand what happened and why, and share the wisdom time has left. This story is imperfect—as all human stories are—but it is offered sincerely, as one person's attempt to contribute.

sense of a path that was at times hopeful, at times painful, but never without purpose.

I am grateful to all who walked beside me—those who challenged me, encouraged me, or bore witness. Each shaped the journey in ways they may never fully know. And to you, the reader, thank you for allowing me the space to tell this story in my own fragile, honest way.

— Sayed Amir Hussain
Lahore, November 2025

PREFACE

In an age defined by noise and distraction, reflection has become an act of courage.

This series, Deep Reflections, was envisioned as a quiet space—an invitation to look inward, to question, and to explore the truths that lie beneath the surface of routine.

The author invites readers not merely to agree or disagree, but to engage each idea with openness, depth, and an honest commitment to self-examination.

May these pages inspire thoughtfulness, humility, and renewed faith.

FOREWORD

The pursuit of reflection is the foundation of all wisdom.

In these pages, the author invites readers to see beyond mere information—to rediscover the art of thinking, feeling, and believing with depth.

Through his words, one senses a devotion to sincerity and inquiry. A rare combination in today's hurried world. This work will speak not only to the intellect but also to the conscience.

May these reflections open pathways to understanding, and may the light of truth continue to guide both reader and writer on their shared journey.

ACKNOWLEDGEMENT

This book's journey owes much to the inspiration and kindness of many. I hold deep gratitude for my parents and teachers, whose wisdom enlightened my early reflections and reasoning.

I deeply appreciate friends and readers who offered thoughtful feedback during the writing process. Their insights reminded me that literature is an enduring dialogue.

Above all, I am thankful for my family, especially my wife Naila, for her steadfast support, and to Allah for granting me the strength and clarity to bring this work to fruition.

—Sayed Amir Hussain

Gratitude is the gentle whisper that follows every genuine act.

TABLE OF CONTENTS

Author's Note... ii
Preface... iv
Foreword... v
Acknowledgement.. vi

Chapter 01 - English: Instructions of Mass Destructions.   1
Chapter 02 - Advertisement 30
Chapter 03 - Is Islam Outdated................................... 38
Chapter 04 - Dare to Teach... 48
Chapter 05 - Why Science and Not Arts..................... 72

Chapter 06 - The Power to Imagine Better................. 78
Chapter 07 - Reading, Culture, and Identity.............. 86
Chapter 08 - Responsibility of Hiring Teachers......... 98

Chapter 09 - The Last 29 106
Chapter 10 - Masculinity.. 112

Chapter 11 - Feminist Agenda.................................... 120
Chapter 12 - The Undermining of Masculinity.......... 130
Chapter 13 - Adult Authority...................................... 138

Afterword.. 146

CHAPTER 1

English – Instructions of Mass Destruction

Part One

"We all agree culture and language are inseparable. This means when a people's culture disappears, their language becomes an orphan, invariably becoming the slave of the replacing culture."

—Dr. Dare Arokoyo

Is it ever right to abandon one's mother tongue for someone else's? It looks like a dreadful betrayal and produces a guilty feeling. How did we arrive at this acceptance—the clear dominance of English in our schools, in our literature, in our culture, and in our politics? Where did it take its route? How did we, as Pakistanis, come to be so feeble towards the claims of our languages on us and so aggressive in our claims on other languages, particularly the language of our colonisation?

I was born in a well-knit family which was closely bound with the community as a whole. The community was like a family where we as children could not do anything wrong, for we would be reported immediately. We spoke Urdu in and outside the home and sometimes Punjabi. I can vividly recall the elders, especially the mothers, narrating religious stories in which everyone was interested and involved. The children's poems like "Joolnay, Tot ba Tot, Chanda Mama Door Kay, Ek Tha Teeter Ek Tha Batair" were a daily diet. We knew our National Anthem and, not only that, but also the song on Kashmir, "Watan Hamara Azad Kashmir". We sang "Lab Pe Aati Hai Dua Ban Ke Tamanna Meri". As we grew a little older, we were told stories of Islamic and national heroes. The next morning, these stories were enthusiastically narrated to other children in our native language. We identified with these stories and realised that the apparently weak can outwit the strong. These stories clearly marked a line between two types of characters: the humans with qualities of courage, kindness, mercy, hatred of evil, and concern for others against the other kind with qualities of greed, selfishness, individualism, and hatred of what was good for the larger co-operative community.

There were good and bad storytellers. A good one could tell the same story over and over again, and it would always be fresh to us, the listeners. He or she could tell a story told by someone else and make it more alive and dramatic. The differences really lay in the use of words and images and the inflexion of voices to effect different tones.

We therefore learnt to value words for their meaning and nuances. Language was not a mere string of words. It had a suggestive power well beyond the immediate and lexical meaning. Our appreciation of the suggestive, magical power of language was reinforced by the games we played with words through riddles, proverbs, the transposition of syllables, or through nonsensical yet musically arranged words. So we learnt the music of our language on top of the content. The language, through images and symbols, gave us a view of the world, but it had a beauty of its own. What was important was that the home, the friends, and the language of the community were one.

And then I went to school—a colonial/missionary school—and this harmony was broken. The language of my education was no longer the language of my culture. English became the language of my formal education. English became more than a language: it was the language, and all the others had to bow before it in deference.

Thus, one of the most humiliating experiences was to be caught speaking Urdu in the vicinity of the school. I was caught speaking Urdu and hence was asked to write 1,000 times that "I will never speak Urdu". I was reported by one of the boys, as children had been encouraged to report. The children were turned into witch-hunters and, in the process, were being taught the lucrative value of being a traitor to one's immediate community.

All the papers were written in English. Nobody could pass the exam who failed the English Language paper, no matter how brilliantly he had done in the other subjects. Thus the most coveted place in the system was only available to the holder of English language brilliance. English became the official vehicle and the magic formula to colonial elitism.

Literary education was now determined by the dominant language while also reinforcing that dominance. Once a month we would walk up to the Mall and excitedly buy Junior Classic comics. Each boy was allotted five comics to buy. These comics were exchanged and read over the month. We were encouraged to read simplified versions of Dickens and Stevenson alongside Rider Haggard. Jim Hawkins, Oliver Twist, Tom Brown—and not any local books—thus our world of imagination became an alien world.

Thus language and literature were taking us further and further from ourselves to other selves, from our world to other worlds. The latest development in speaking English is copying the original accent; pronunciation with accent has become a norm. We all agree that no culture (and therefore language) is inferior to any other. Then why do most intellectuals promoting the English language impose Western cultures (dress, dance, architecture, literature) on us?

Of course, English is spoken the world over, but in most countries it is just a language of communication. In our country it is a carrier of their culture. Culture embodies those moral, ethical, and aesthetic values through which people come to view themselves and their place in the universe. Values are the basis of a people's identity, their sense of particularity as members of the human race. All this is carried by language. Language as culture is the collective memory bank of a people's experience in history. But its most important area of domination was the mental universe of the colonised: the control, through culture, of how people perceived themselves and their relationship to the world. To control a people's culture is to control their tools of self-definition in relationship to others.

It began with the East India Company stepping on the subcontinent with one common refrain—to make quick money at the expense of the children of the soil. They were known as the original corporate raiders. For a century, the East India Company conquered and plundered vast tracts of South Asia. They entrenched themselves in the subcontinent.

It did not take long for the Hindus and Muslims to realise the Company was exploiting the country at the cost of Hindustan. The riches of India were drained out to the British Empire. India was left to itself. The hatred for the Company began to grow. It was at this time Sir Charles Trevelyan—brother-in-law of Macaulay—speaking on the Muslims, said they regarded the British rulers as "kafirs", as infidel usurpers, and the Hindus regarded them as *mlecchas* (impure barbarians) with whom no communion was to be held. Both Muslims and Hindus thought they had been excluded from avenues of wealth and distinction, and the corporate raiders gained everything.

The cunning Macaulay then carved out a clever plan for their benefit: to impart education to the "heathen" of India. He thought of educating some of the influential Indians and thereby winning the confidence of the upper classes to consolidate British rule in India. A new policy of education was adopted which was popularly known as the "Filtration Theory". The fundamental assumption of this theory was that higher education, if provided to the top classes, would somehow or other "filter down to the masses", because culture and enlightenment always filter from upper classes to the lower and not vice versa. It therefore advocated the view that the government should concentrate its energy and resources on educating the upper classes who in turn would educate the lower. Hence, this concept of class education—as clearly distinguished from mass education—stood as a stumbling block to the substantial progress of education in general.

His idea whether to continue the institutions of Oriental learning was dismissed, as he held the view that they did not serve any useful purpose. With regard to the medium of instruction, the claim of mother tongue was dismissed on the grounds that the spoken dialects contained neither literature nor scientific information and were "so poor and rude that until they are enriched from some other source, it will not be easy to translate any work into them." He did not know either Sanskrit or Arabic. In utter dislike and out of sheer vanity, he had the audacity to assert that "a single shelf of a good European library was worth the whole native literature of India and Arabia". So Sanskrit and Arabic had no claim as the medium of instruction. "In India, English is the language spoken by the ruling class. It is spoken by the higher class of natives at the seats of government." So English should be taught in the best interests of India.

Macaulay then strongly recommended that the aim of educational policy in India should be to spread Western learning through the medium of the English language. He also suggested that existing institutions of Oriental learning should be used for the promotion of English education and remarked, "Indians will be taught what is good for their health and not palatable to their dishes."

His rationale behind the argument in adopting this educational policy was to create "a class of persons, Indian in blood and colour, but English in taste, in opinions, in morals, and in intellect". His real motive was the cultural dominance of the people of India. He shrewdly provided the Company English-conversant Indians for holding petty jobs in the office of the Company and at the same time reduced the Company's administrative expenses. It was clear that the "Downward Filtration Theory" further divided the already divided people of India and added a new class to the one which already existed. From then on, no stipend was given to any student entering Oriental institutions, and not a morsel of funds was to be spent on printing Oriental works.

The real intention of Macaulay is best revealed from a letter which he had written to his father and which has been quoted by Major B D Basu in his book *Education in India Under the East India Company*. The letter says: "The effect of this education on the Hindus is prodigious. No Hindu who has received English education ever remains sincerely attached to his religion. It is my firm belief that if our plans of education are followed up, there will not be a single idolater among the respectable classes in Bengal thirty years hence." This clearly reveals his real intention—to undermine the religious, social, and cultural heritage of India with a view to securing complete cultural conquest.

The demand for English education increased in higher and middle-class societies. It was a slow but sure process: the customs and traditions began to crumble and people's minds began to change. The English language had conquered the minds of the people. It was even introduced in government-sponsored colleges which provided education in Oriental subjects. English had taken a giant leap in replacing the local languages.

–End of Part 1–

English – Instructions of Mass Destruction

Part Two

By the time my generation was admitted to school, English had firmly entrenched itself. We were not allowed to speak in our native language. Speaking in Urdu or any other local language in school was forbidden. I was eight years old when I was admitted to boarding school. I did not know a word of English; even then, I was punished for conversing in the vernacular. I was asked to write a thousand lines: "I will never speak in Urdu." It was Sunday morning when academic detention was carried out under the supervision of a teacher—ironically, a Pakistani Urdu-speaking lady who taught us Urdu and Islamiat. She was the only Pakistani teacher; the rest were all foreigners—sisters, brothers, and fathers. At that age, I did not understand the psychological ramifications of the English language, nor language as a weapon and a site of intense neocolonial conflict.

Soon my friends and I became fervent exponents of the English language. We quickly abandoned our indigenous languages and became adept in English within some months. We were told that English would enhance international communication—for example, with people living on the other side of the globe—and that through the use of a European language we would gain recognition and even financial reward from a worldwide audience.

We are now so obsessed with English that a city like Karachi, where educated Urdu-speaking people have settled, is happy speaking in English with their children. Those who cannot converse in English try to talk to their children in broken English. The city has rejected its mother tongue for the sake of worldly goods. Ironically, those who had the responsibility to hold the language together are themselves ashamed to speak in their mother tongue.

With this background, the question arises: why did we not devise ways to replace English? Our tragedy has been that our own people at the helm of affairs did not want it to happen. These English-speaking and foreign-qualified Pakistani bureaucrats-cum-educationists vehemently advocated for English to be the medium of instruction—the privileged ones whom God ordained the education of elites.

They showed census figures as progress of education in Pakistan, but without realising that it may be of no importance to the people of Pakistan to boast today of many times as many "educated" members as in 1947. If they are the wrong kind, the increase in numbers will be a disadvantage rather than an advantage. The only question which concerns us here is whether these "educated" persons are actually equipped to face the ordeal before them, or whether they unconsciously contribute to their own undoing by perpetuating the regime of the oppressor.

Herein, however, lies no argument for the oft-heard contention that education for the West should mean one thing and for us a different thing. It is merely a matter of exercising common sense in approaching people through their environment in order to deal with conditions as they are, rather than as we would like to see them or imagine them to be. There may be a different method of attack, but the principle remains the same.

Highly educated Pakistanis denounce persons who advocate an education different from that given to the West. We who have been disadvantaged for so long and denied opportunities for development are naturally afraid of anything that sounds like discrimination. We are anxious to have everything these people have recommended, even if it is harmful.

The possibility of originality in Pakistan loses credibility one hundred per cent in attempting to maintain a nominal equality. If the colonial masters decide to take up Mormonism, we must follow their lead. If they reject such a study, then we must do likewise. Why can't we develop and carry out a programme of our own? If the colonial masters want to hold a faulty system, let them do so.

The modern education system has been devised to imprison the minds of the uneducated, but it does them much good because it has been worked out in line with the needs of those who have enslaved the downtrodden, weaker peoples. As a result, the philosophy and ethics emanating from our educational system have justified slavery, peerage, segregation, and lynching. The oppressor has the right to exploit, to handicap, and to kill the oppressed. We are daily educated in the tenets of such a religion of the strong, and have accepted the status of the weak as divinely ordained. During the last three generations of their nominal freedom, they have done practically nothing to change it. Their pointing and resolutions indulged in by a few have been of little avail.

We had a practical example of this in the biggest college in Pakistan—branded as the institution of all institutions—which suddenly, out of nowhere, had a foreign principal whose arrogance and aggressiveness literally silenced everyone. He realised the nation is impressed by the white skin and would yield to whatever he said. He bullied the dissenting parents in a gathering by outrightly telling them to withdraw their children if they didn't like the policy of the school. When the discipline dropped, he warned teachers and parents not to mention a word about it; he choked them into silence. The parents and teachers, knowing quite well that he was a petty tyrant, kept themselves quiet. The teachers were so cowed down by his attitude that they kept all secrets to themselves. Nobody ever discussed his administrative abuse, though among their close circle they described him as "an individual who lords his power over others, acts in an arbitrary and self-aggrandising manner, belittles subordinates, evidences lack of consideration, discourages initiative, and utilises non-contingent punishment." "Abusive disrespect," a concept developed by him, included deceit, constraint, coercion, selfishness, inequity, cruelty, disregard, and false praise. A typical example of a Pakistani mind brought under the control of the oppressor.

The problem of holding us down, therefore, is easily solved. When you control a man's thinking, you do not have to worry about his actions—you do not have to tell him not to stand here or go yonder. He will find his "proper place" and will stay in it. You do not need to send him to the back door. He will go without being told. In fact, if there is no back door, he will cut one out for his special benefit. His education makes it necessary.

I saw a clear example of this at Lahore Airport. Here was a woman who had an argument with a security officer. The argument was loud and aggressive, though one could easily feel the woman was in the wrong. The woman who was hostile and belligerent in Pakistan became cringing and servile at Houston Airport. There was a visible change in her—she had come to the land of the masters.

Women who are educated in English-medium schools are like the oppressors—those who inspire and stimulate the oppressors with the thought that they are everything and have accomplished everything worthwhile—yet they depress and crush us by making us feel that we do not amount to much and never will measure up to the standards of the educated. Thus a Pakistani educated in this way becomes a hopeless liability to us.

The difficulty is that an educated Pakistani is compelled to move among his own people, whom he has been taught to despise. As a rule, the educated Pakistani has been taught that the common Pakistani is not clean. It does not matter how often a commoner washes his hands; he remains dirty anyway. And it does not matter how often a European man uses his hands; he cannot soil them. Ironically, when the same people serve as domestic servants, it does not matter how dirty they are.

-End of Part 2-

English – Instructions of Mass Destruction

Part Three

The "educated Pakistani" has the attitude of contempt toward his own people because he is taught to admire English. They are made to read "classics" along with books taught in classes. Their teachers—even those teaching Islamiat—advocate the superiority of the white race. Pakistani schools become places where inferiority is reinforced—they must be convinced of their inferiority. I know of an incident where a student had written about Jihad in the Cambridge Examination; the school was promptly intimated by the white masters to keep an eye on the boy. The boy's parents were told to tone down the 'aggressiveness' of the child. Imagine the level of control exercised over us, and the level of obedience displayed by us.

This thought of inferiority is drilled into us in almost every class. A boy goes back home where parents innocently repeat that the child's future lies in foreign soil. A large majority of our educated people, on the verge of completing their schooling, are all but worthless for us—yet ready to serve another nation. If after leaving school they have the opportunity to serve the nation by living, teaching, or preaching what they have been taught, they never become a constructive force in the development of the country. This becomes the questionable factor in the life of the despised people.

When a student has finished his education in our schools, he has been equipped to begin the life of an Americanised or Europeanised man. Yet before he steps from the threshold of his alma mater, he is told by his teachers that he must return to his own people—people from whom he has been estranged by a vision of ideals which, in his disillusionment, he will realise he cannot attain. The people whom he has been ordered to serve have been belittled by his teachers to such an extent that he can hardly find delight in undertaking what his education has led him to believe is impossible. He resigns himself to becoming another imitator. He becomes sour in life—too pessimistic—unable to be a constructive force; and thus usually develops into a chronic fault-finder.

In their imitation, these "educated people" are sincere. They intend to bridge the gap existing between the so-called educated and the enthusiastic masses ready to follow—yet not realising that nothing new will be accomplished. They will simply add to the number of imitators.

These "educated people" vilify their own language, their own literature, their own culture, poetry, art, and Pakistani thought. Some, in subtle ways, denounce their own religion—"bigot" is already a common word used. You are immediately labelled a militant hardliner the moment you mention religion. Frankly speaking, we must concede that these things do not exist for them. These things did not figure in the courses they pursued in school—and why would they? When we emphasise these things, we invite racial discrimination by recognising such differences between Europeans and us—differences that would justify segregation. We fail to see that it is not us who take this position; it is they who force us into it. Difference in culture does not mean superiority or inferiority. It indicates that everyone has certain gifts which others do not possess. By developing these gifts, they justify their right to exist.

People who maintained schools for education were certainly sincere. These earnest workers, however, had more enthusiasm than knowledge. They did not understand the task before them. Their understanding amounted more to an effort toward social uplift than actual education. Their aim was to transform the people rather than develop them. Instead of enlightening their thought, they followed traditional curricula which did not consider the people except to condemn or pity them.

The question arises: why have many of those who serve as teachers not been able to effect change? These teachers, however, are powerless. They have no control over our education and have little voice in matters pertaining to it. Some have been chosen as members of public boards of education, and some appointed members of private boards, yet these members have no influence in the final working out of the educational programme. Education—hence the most important thing in the uplift of the people—is almost entirely in the hands of those who have enslaved and now segregate us.

With "wrongly educated people" in control of themselves, it is doubtful that the system would be very different from what it is, or that it would rapidly undergo change. Those placed in charge would be the products of the same system and would show no more conception of the task at hand than the masters and enslavers who educated them and shaped their minds as they wished them to function.

We may have more sympathy and interest in our people than our colonial masters now exploiting our institutions as educators. Yet taught from books of the same bias, trained by the British possessing the same prejudices—or by wrongly educated Pakistanis of enslaved minds—one generation of Pakistanis after another has served no higher purpose than to do what they are told to do. In other words, a Pakistani teacher instructing Pakistani children is in many respects a British colonial teacher, for the programme in each case is the same. They scoff at the national language and have been taught to scorn rather than understand their own linguistic history—which is certainly more important for them than the study of English, French, German, Spanish, or any other foreign language.

A pertinent question may be asked: why have Pakistanis who serve their nation as teachers not changed this programme? The answer is simple: these teachers are powerless and in need of a job. They have no control over their education and have little voice in matters pertaining to it. In most cases, teachers often perceive abusive or harmful behaviour as the status quo; they become socialised into accepting abusive behaviour from administrators, not realising they have a right to fair and respectful treatment. The education of Pakistanis—then the most important thing in our uplift—is almost entirely in the hands of those who have enslaved and now segregate them.

With "desi angrez" in control, it is doubtful that the system would be much different or change swiftly. The "desi angrez" placed in charge are the products of the same system and show no more conception of the task at hand than their masters who educated and shaped them. We may have more sympathy and interest in our people than the British, American, Australian, or New Zealand educators now exploiting our institutions, but we too lack the vision of our competitors. Taught from books of the same bias, trained by foreigners of the same prejudices or by Pakistanis of enslaved minds, one generation of "desi teachers" after another has served no higher purpose than to do as they are told. In other words, a "desi teacher" instructing our children is in many respects a foreign teacher, for the programme in each case is about the same. The present system under foreign control trains the "desis" in the ways of foreign masters, and at the same time convinces them of the impropriety or impossibility of becoming white. It compels the "desi" to become a good Pakistani—yet for the performance of which his education is ill-suited. The British exploit us through economic restriction and segregation, all the while considering the present system sound.

Haven't we seen the mushroom growth of English-medium schools in Pakistan? In more than forty years of my career, I have seen school heads berating teachers for wearing hijab in school, humiliating them in front of others so that everyone realises they should not do likewise. These Europeanised heads and teachers are abundant—they have penetrated the remotest areas of Pakistan where wearing hijab is a way of life, and they are trying to train people as their masters have instructed them. The school heads have given boys and girls a free hand to mix to the extent of going beyond the limits set by our culture. When I, as a headmaster, tried to control the situation, I was told that if I enforced discipline by checking boys and girls, the school might lose students to other branches. I stood firm. I had read somewhere:

"We must be uncompromising in our vigilance; we must be unyielding in our resolve." A. C. Benson wrote about maintaining discipline: "It insults the soul; it is destructive of all self-respect and dignity to be incessantly at the mercy of boys. They are merciless, and the pathos of the situation never touches them at all." I then resolved to crack down on the discipline of the school. A dangerous ground to tread on, I met stiff resistance, for "highly educated" Pakistanis do not like to hear anything uttered against this procedure, because they make their living through it and feel compelled to defend the system. Few teachers ever dare act otherwise; and if they express themselves, they are easily crushed by the large majority so that the procession may move without interruption.

It took about four months to bring the situation under control. It was most heartening to receive appreciation from the parents. They were grateful to the school for changing the attitude of the students and for aligning the school with the culture of our country. The students were happy to come to school, and teachers were pleased that serious work was being done during school hours.

–End of Part 3–

English – Instructions of Mass Destruction

Part Four

Once a year a group of professionals are sent from the Cambridge University to train the School Heads. The School Heads, after attending these conferences, are in a state of Nirvana. They return to their schools eager to implement the latest methods of teaching used in England. They blindly follow the methods and force the teachers to do the same. The teachers, too, slavishly follow the herd, for we have been taught that our masters can serve us more efficiently in these spheres. I have attended a number of such conferences, within and outside the country, sponsored by the British Council and Cambridge University. A group of highly qualified luminaries is there to enlighten us in the latest methods of teaching. The participants have to cough up a large sum in order to become more "original" in teaching. We are thus reduced to teaching and preaching. We will have no outlet but to go down a blind alley if the sort of education we are receiving is to enable us to find the way out of our present difficulties. We will never be able to show originality as long as our efforts are directed from without by those who socially forbid us. Such "friends" will unconsciously keep us in the gutter.

Unfortunately, those who dare to express themselves

are branded as opponents of interracial cooperation. As a matter of fact, however, such persons are the real workers in carrying out a programme of interracial effort. Cooperation implies equality of the participants in the particular task at hand. On the contrary, however, the usual way now is for Cambridge to work out their plans behind closed doors, have them approved by a few enslaved and influential Pakistani owners of school chains serving nominally on a board, and then employ a white or mixed staff to carry out their programme. The story doesn't end here. All the English-medium schools in Pakistan spend a handsome amount to get this first-hand knowledge from the white masters. This is not interracial cooperation. It is merely the ancient idea of calling upon the "inferior" to carry out the orders of the "superior." As Jessie O. Thomas, a black American, expressed: "We do the 'coing' and the whites the 'operating.'"

This unsound attitude of the "friends" of Pakistanis is due to the persistence of the mediaeval idea of controlling underprivileged classes. Behind closed doors these "friends" say you need to be careful in advancing these Pakistani people to commanding positions unless it can be determined beforehand that they will do what they are told to do. You can never tell when some Pakistanis will break out and embarrass their "friends." After being advanced to positions of influence, some of them have been known to run amok and advocate social equality or demand for their people the privileges of democracy when they should restrict themselves to education and religious development.

We have not been qualified to administer our own affairs. Those qualified must be foreign qualified. It was with this in mind that Musharraf, the President of Pakistan, inducted foreign-qualified state ministers in his cabinet; Imran Khan followed suit. Both governments failed ingloriously. If we develop replicas of Harvard, Yale, Columbia, and Princeton—if these are top graduates of our country who have not touched the life of the ordinary people—the money thus invested goes to waste. These institutions have produced three types of people: some become more adept in the exploitation of their people; a smaller number may cross the divide and join their masters in useful service; but the large majority of the products of such institutions will increase rather than diminish the load which the masses have had to carry since partition. Such ill-prepared workers will have no foundation upon which to build.

I keep hearing from highly educated students of mine that we need institutions like LUMS with professors qualified from foreign universities—sadly out of touch with the people and their own culture. In other words, you can build a multi-million-dollar institution and place a foreigner in charge to do what you want to accomplish. He is given the responsibility to hire and train the men necessary to make a university. Can universities be established with such raw recruits? Then you think of doctorates. It dawned upon me—the degradation of the doctorate—when an acquaintance of mine came to me trying to extract my sympathies. "I just failed to get a job for which I had been working, and I am told that I cannot expect a promotion until I get my 'darkter's 'gree.'" That is what he called it. He could not even pronounce the words, but he is determined to have his "darkter's 'gree" to get the job in sight.

This shameful status of higher education is due in large measure to low standards of institutions with a tendency toward the diploma-mill procedure. To get a job or to hold one, you go in and stay until they "grind" you out a "darkter's 'gree." And you do not have to worry any further. The assumption is that almost any school will be glad to have you thereafter, and you will receive a large salary.

Investigations have shown, however, that men who have the doctorate degree not only lose touch with the common people, but do not do as much creative work as those of less formal education. After having this honour conferred upon them, these so-called scholars often go off to sleep. Hardly any seriousness is shown later to this inertia among men who are put in the lead of things because of meeting the statutory requirements of frontier universities which are not on the frontier.

We offer no argument here against earning advanced degrees, but these should come as honours conferred for training crowned with scholastic distinction—not to enable a man to increase his salary or find a better-paying position. One of the crimes of such education as received by us is that we thereby learn little as to making a living. From the perspective of non-whites, it is as if, in the last so many centuries, white Europeans exploded a "cultural bomb" all over the world, diminishing the value of non-white people and their ways—through colonisation, imperialism, industrialisation, and globalisation.

The effect of the cultural bomb is to annihilate a people's belief in their names, in their languages, in their environment, in their heritage of struggle, in their unity, in their capacities, and ultimately in themselves. It makes them see their past as one wasteland of non-achievement, and it makes them want to distance themselves from that wasteland. It makes them want to identify with that which is furthest removed from themselves—for instance, with other peoples' languages rather than their own. It makes them identify with that which is decadent and reactionary—all those forces that would stop their own springs of life. It even plants serious doubts about the moral righteousness of struggle. Possibilities of triumph or victory are seen as remote, ridiculous dreams. The intended results are despair, despondency, and a collective death-wish.

Excerpt from Ngũgĩ wa Thiong'o,
Decolonising the Mind:
The Politics of Language in African Literature (1986).

"When a people lose their language, they do not learn another—they lose themselves."

CHAPTER 2

Advertisements: The Mercenary Display of Brainwashing

The article by one of our former Middle School English teachers inspired me to write on the influence of Movies and Television ads on our younger generation. I will confine myself, at first, to American ads. I intend to write about the ads playing on Pakistani television later.

Author Frank Peretti coined the term "wounded spirits" and used it as the title of his excellent book based on his own childhood experience. He was born with a tumour in his jaw that disfigured him and led to unmerciful taunting during his childhood. He saw himself as a "monster," because that is what he was called by other children. Frank is joined by millions of others who have been through years of rejection and ridicule because of a physical abnormality or unsightly characteristic.

This vulnerability to one's peers has always been part of the human experience, but today's children and teens are even more sensitive to it. The reason is that popular culture has become a tyrannical master that demands ever-greater conformity to its shifting ideal of perfection. For example, if you have had an occasion to watch an old Elvis Presley movie, you must have noticed that the girls who were paraded in bikinis were slightly overweight and out of shape. There they were, "twisting" their corpulent behinds to the delight of Elvis and the other oversexed members of his band. But those actresses who seemed so luscious in 1960 could not make it on Baywatch today. Most of them would need to spend a year or two in the gym and undergo breast augmentation to make the grade. In Rembrandt's day, the women considered exceptionally beautiful were downright fat. Today, extreme thinness and "hard bodies" have become the ideal, sometimes bordering on masculinity. In short, the standard of perfection has shifted upward and been placed out of reach for most kids.

The media and the entertainment industry are largely responsible for the assault we are witnessing today. They laud images of bodily perfection, including "supermodels," "playmates," "babes," and "hunks." The net effect on children and teens is profound, not only in America but around the world. We saw it illustrated dramatically when Western satellite TV transmission penetrated the islands of the South Pacific for the first time. It projected images of gorgeous, very thin actresses who starred on Melrose Place, Beverly Hills 90210, and other teen-oriented shows. Four years later, a survey of sixty-five Fijian girls revealed how their attitudes had been shaped (or warped) by what they had seen. Almost immediately, the girls began to dress and try to fix their hair like Western women. The beauty cult is an international curse plaguing hundreds of millions of people, most of them young, with a sense of inferiority.

Another key factor is the prevalence of violence in the media, which has taught kids the wrong way to deal with tormentors. Teens, including those with wounded spirits, live every day with images of killing, poisoning, maiming, decapitating, knifing, crashing, and exploding. It is everywhere, from the theatre to cable television to music videos and Internet. One of the most popular movies a few years ago was Scream, produced by Miramax—a subsidiary owned, it is sad to say, by the Disney Corporation. The film opened with the brutal killing of a young girl. Her body was then disembowelled and left hanging on a clothesline to be discovered by her mother. Millions of teenagers saw this movie during their most impressionable years. Scream 2 and Scream 3 have come along since. Thanks, Disney, for doing this to our kids. Your founder would roll in his grave if he knew what you are doing with his good name. So go ahead. Take the money and run. But as you go, remember that the blood of innocent victims will stain your hands forever. I deeply resent this demoralisation and exploitation of the young that Disney Chairman and other movie television moguls have perpetrated at the expense of the most impressionable among us.

Given the pervasiveness of violence in the media, why are we surprised when kids who have seen and heard it throughout childhood sometimes act in violent ways? Children are taught that killing is the way they are supposed to act when insulted or frustrated. Because popular culture has taught them that violence is manly. Wasn't Sylvester Stallone violent in Rambo? Wasn't Bruce Willis violent in Die Hard? Wasn't Arnold Schwarzenegger violent in Commando? Aren't our boys learning from these role models to get even or to kill those who get in their way?

Protecting the family from this culture of violence is very difficult for parents. It's like trying to hold back the falling rain. Nevertheless, we must shield our kids from it as much as possible, especially when they are young.

Therefore, when we teach children kindness and respect for others by insisting on civility in our classrooms and in our homes, we're laying a foundation for human kindness in the world of adulthood to come.

There was a time parents had a better understanding of the need for an orderly progression through childhood. Kids in that day were given plenty of time to play and giggle and be themselves. There were cultural "markers" that determined the ages at which certain behaviours were appropriate. Boys, for example, wore short pants until they were twelve or thirteen. Now those markers have disappeared, or they have been moved downward. Children are depicted on TV as having more insight and maturity than their elders. They are rushed, ready or not, from the womb to the nursery school to the adult world at breakneck pace. This scurrying to maturity leaves a child without a strong foundation on which to build because it takes time to build a healthy human being. When you rush your kids, they have to deal with sexual and peer pressures for which their young minds are not prepared. There is another problem with making children grow up too quickly. When you treat them as though they are adults, it becomes more difficult to set limits on their adolescent behaviour down the road. How can you establish a curfew for a thirteen-year-old rebel who has been taught to think of himself as your peer?

All sane men who condemn us will be condemned forever. Our only goods are handsome young men. We adhere to a cult of beauty, moral and aesthetic. All that is ugly and vulgar and banal will be annihilated.

Disrespect for men pervades the entertainment industry, including many television commercials. The formula involves a beautiful woman (or a bevy of them) who is intelligent, sexy, admirable, and self-assured. She encounters a slob of a man, usually in a bar, who is a braggart—ignorant, balding, and overweight. The stupid "you", as I will call him, quickly disgraces himself on screen, at which point the woman sneers or walks away. There are hundreds of these ads on TV today. Watch for them on the tube. They are constantly changing, but this is the kind of stuff you will see:

The Internet has become a never-ending source of humour directed against men. Here is another example from an anonymous author, called Dumb Men Jokes—Strange but True. It isn't very funny, but it makes the point.

1. Don't imagine you can change a man—unless he's in nappies.
2. Never let your man's mind wander—it's too little to be out alone.
3. Definition of a bachelor: a man who has missed the opportunity to make some woman miserable.
4. Best way to get a man to do something: suggest he is too old for it.
5. If you want a committed man, look in a mental hospital.
6. Go for a younger man. You might as well—they never mature anyway.
7. What's the best way to force a man to do sit-ups? Put the remote control between his toes.
8. If a man belittles a woman, it could become a lawsuit. But if women belittle men, it's a Hallmark card.

My greatest concern is for vulnerable, impressionable boys and what is being done to them. They, like their dads, are the objects of societal scorn today. Please let me give the greatest emphasis to this point: Not only do radical feminists and elitists tell us that men are fools but that boys are fools too. They are universal scapegoats, the clumsy clods with smelly feet who care only about sports and mischief. Harvard psychologist William Pollack said women consider boys to be creatures who might "infect girls with some kind of social cooties".

Tailpiece:

In a nationwide TV programme one of the finals of the national spelling bee competition, the first, second and third place winners had each been home-schooled. The winner looked at the camera and thanked God that He had given him the ability to compete. His father was even more impressive. He said to the interviewer, "I'm proud of what my son has accomplished. He did a good job. But I'm much more pleased about the development of his character than I am his intellectual accomplishments."

"The beauty cult is an international curse plaguing hundreds of millions of young people with a sense of inferiority."

CHAPTER 3

Is Islam Outdated?

Keeping your word was a sacred thing at home. My dad used to say, "The only thing a poor man has is his word. It's the one thing nobody can take from you." I was told by my mother that treating people with integrity and respect is the only way to get them to achieve their full potential. Remember, character and integrity, if divorced from God, do not make sense. If you try to set your own moral thermostat, chances are that a lot of other people will be uncomfortable. What was she trying to instil in us? I understood this after a long time: integrity left to define itself becomes evil because everyone ends up choosing his own standards. Such profound thoughts could not be appreciated at that immature age; we took them lightly as they were coming from a mother who was not highly educated. We had been taught in school by our teachers to reason out everything. These thoughts were in conflict with my mother's ideas.

Those who believe God created humans have a different worldview from those who believe humans created God. Are we here to have nature serve us, or are we here because we are to serve nature? Politics are totally directed by worldview. That's why when people say, "We ought to separate politics from religion," I say separating the two is absolutely impossible.

When Man Becomes God:

Public debate today is filled with arguments that, not long ago, would have been dismissed as ridiculous and insupportable. Consider homosexuality, for instance. There have been homosexuals in every human culture. But until recently, who would have dared to suggest that the practice should be accepted on equal footing with heterosexuality, to be thought of as a personal decision and nothing more?

Abortion also became acceptable because we decided it is acceptable. Where did we get the right to make that decision? Because we're our own god. If the inconvenience of this little child would interrupt our college education or a relationship with a boyfriend or girlfriend, then that child becomes nothing more than a choice. "It's my choice. I decide for myself. What about me?" That is the essence of the culture. I have my own career to make; children will be an impediment to my success, so why have them? It becomes a matter of choice. We have set our standards.

Everything comes down to the faith question, which then leads to the integrity question: Where does integrity of character come from? Either it comes from God or it comes from something we manufacture. If it comes from God, it is fixed. Of course, in practice we will invariably fall short of perfection, but our practice will always push against a fixed absolute—the standard that is the same today, yesterday, and forever. The standard my grandfather had will be the same standard my grandchildren will have. We may pull away from it further and more often, but the standard stays.

If I don't believe there is a God, then I don't believe

character is fixed. I believe it moves as the culture moves. Therefore, what was wrong once is no longer wrong because the culture no longer considers it inappropriate; we are able to move the standards. The ancient landmark or boundary stone set by our forefathers means that once you move your reference point, everything else becomes chaos.

The educated people believe that if someone makes an innocent mistake where his intentions were good, you are afraid to define what is right and wrong. They would say, "You'll have to find out for yourself," or "Do whatever seems good to you." They tell them, "It doesn't matter what you believe as long as you are sincere." Such misguided sentiments are the tragic product of our relativistic generation. We believe fairness is more important than accuracy, that effort counts more than excellence, that participation is as good as achievement. We are scared to death to say, "That's wrong." We try to excuse it. "He was just expressing himself. Don't squash his creativity!" But children need to be disciplined and to know there are lines they must live within.

An aeroplane has a chalked-out path it has to fly within—that allotted funnel chosen for it. It doesn't ever go off course. The air traffic controller directs the pilot. He has to be kept within limits or else he may lead to disaster. The Motorway Authority advises you through signboards to keep in your lane, for it may be hazardous for you. Don't we check kids to stop them fiddling with electric switches? Is it narrow-minded to limit them to that one path? Similarly, our children must be told what is safe or else they court disaster.

We refuse to direct our children and then run around moaning, "What is wrong with our kids today? Look at the violence! Look at the decadence! Look at the drug addiction and lack of respect!" Why are we moaning? We trained them to be this way. They have become critical about everything; public officials fail the integrity test. The media is saturated with it. The reason for this, I believe, is that by showing the character flaws in other people, the public affirms that its own inadequacies are really not so abnormal. As the character of Pakistan begins to plummet, we want to justify our own lack of morality by somehow showing that everyone is just as bad.

People who lie think everyone is a liar. Thieves think everyone steals. People who are insincere in their comments and actions think everyone else is insincere. Therefore, people who are essentially unethical think everyone is unethical, and they're determined to find it in you. If you're not overtly flawed, you become a contrast and a threat. Men are lovers of darkness rather than light because the light exposes their dark deeds.

I remember when I was in school there was a 10 p.m. lights-out policy. As soon as the lights were off and the prefect was sleeping, the boys would get up, fish out their hidden eatables and transistors. When the prefect heard something and switched on the lights, everybody would scramble around like cockroaches and jump into the nearest bed. In the dark, we misbehaved; in the light, we hid in fear.

That's what has happened to the public at large. People are desperate to justify their own immoral attitudes by saying, "He's a failure too, so I'm as good as he is." Our generation has learned to hold to the standard of each other instead of the standard of God. That is the travesty: God is no longer the standard; we are. It is this which has caused problems with everything from discipline in the schools to pornography on the Internet.

How did it happen? I got a job in one of the largest chains of schools in Pakistan. On the first day I realised the prayer was taken out of the morning assembly. That's a simplistic answer but then even the National Anthem was missing; nobody among the staff realised that these were part of the morning assembly. But when the prayers were introduced, the children were not interested, and with the National Anthem there were giggles and chuckles. Slowly girls and boys came to me and appreciated the effort; they had been told by their parents that they must talk to me on their behalf as well. It was with some effort the students became serious. But it wasn't just the prayer in schools; it wasn't just television; it wasn't just corruption; it wasn't just welfare; it wasn't just mobile phones. It wasn't any one thing.

The only way to destroy something with a solid foundation is to chip away at it, one value at a time. Take away its heart and essence. Bring doubt to what used to be confidence, denial to what used to be faith, death to what was life. I think that is what has happened.

Contrast the generation of the '50s and '60s with the generation of today. In those days people were tentative about the new country; they were poor, hungry, and out of work. Hunger could easily have been justified by saying, "I'm hungry, and I don't have as much as you; therefore, I have a right to take what I can get." Dishonesty was still considered wrong, and thieves were despised. Our problems do not result from economics or deficiencies in education. They result from the selfish decision to ignore God's standards of integrity. Standards based on anything else are relative, and relative standards are meaningless.

When I came back to the school I had been in for 26 years, I noticed how far the school had drifted, one tiny step at a time. My antenna was attuned to school life to notice the small changes that had taken place. Instead, I experienced firsthand school reform gone terribly wrong. Students who did nothing were passed, and students who did nothing more than cut and paste from Wikipedia were deemed high performers. Disruptive students were permitted to rob their classmates of precious teaching time.

When I pointed out the flaws, I was faced with taunting remarks by no less than the Principal. The school assembly, a sacred event in the morning, was hit hard. As a headmaster I was told to wait till the assembly was ready. When I went, there was chaos: boys were all over the place, and the assembly quadrangle was noisy. I stood there for a while then enquired from the deputy head if that was a daily routine. His answer was, "Sir, at the start of the prayers they'll be quiet." Thank God they did, but it had never been like this. Boys were always quiet at assembly time, waiting for the head to start the assembly. Boys are never at fault; it's the elders who give them a chance to misbehave. When the boys were told of the century-old tradition, they began to behave. The resolve to do right, regardless of the circumstances or of the consequences, was the issue.

The Great Influence:

In our journey to life, each one of us is the product of many influences, some major, some less important. It's like my friend used to say about the boarding house food. If there were more Aloo than Qeema, then let's call it Aloo

Qeema; if there were more qeema, then call it qeema aloo. So what does that mean? Every ingredient makes a difference. When it is all finished, a unique flavour results. Many people have been key ingredients in my life. The first ones were my parents, the working-class people who struggled to make ends meet but who were grateful for what they had and made the most of it. They had a better life than their parents, but they wanted a better life for their children. They worked hard and carefully instilled a solid work ethic in their children, insisting that no one was going to hand us anything—we had to work for it. My father was very clear in his mind: "Nobody is going to speak in English at home, as your mother doesn't understand it." These instructions were given because he sent us to the best of schools whose job was to teach us English; he didn't want us to forget our culture. He had thought then that English, being the language of the masters, was gradually penetrating into our culture.

My mother was probably the most community-minded person I have ever known. Whenever there was need, she would run to help. If there was some little girl who was desperately ill and needed special treatment, she would see to it. She had the knack of collecting ladies from the community, knitting them into a family, allocating work to each individual lady, and making them work like a well-oiled machine. She was a great believer that one should give something back to the community.

I grew up in this small orthodox community. At the time, the theology that dominated was somewhat legalistic. Although today I believe this emphasis is misguided, it probably protected me from dangerous experiments that damaged peers.

The other side of the coin was that there was a

heavy emphasis on the study of the Quran and memorisation, but before I could benefit from it I was sent to a boarding school. Even then my mother had a big influence on me. Prior to my departure, she made me understand the value of some of the holy verses. As I grew I became more inquisitive and liked to ask questions about "Why can't we?" or "Why is it wrong?" I was not satisfied when the answers were, "You're just not supposed to." Being away from home I was not given satisfactory answers.

"Well, why? Why is that wrong?"

"Because...it's just not the way we are supposed to do it."

When I was fourteen or fifteen, I went through a period of disenchantment with such non-answers. I know it's tempting to say, "Because the Holy Book says it's wrong," and leave it at that. But there are reasons why the Book says it's wrong, and there are rational, appropriate foundations for the prohibitions we find in God's word. Part of my rebellion was toward this "can't do" mentality. I wanted to know what I could do. Tell me something that is positive; tell me something that is worthy of my life, something I can invest myself in. Don't just give a list of restrictions!

My own experience has taught me that we can't get by with telling teenagers "just because!" when it comes to spiritual matters. We need to give them the principles behind the rules. They may not agree with them, but at least we have given them a basis to understand the "why" when we tell them not to drink or whatever.

My early struggle with legalism greatly affected my walk with God. Today I am definitely a "grace Muslim" and not a "law Muslim." One of the few things I detest more than liberalism is legalism. I think both are cancers to the Muslim faith—liberalism because it doesn't believe anything, and legalism because it restricts us only to the things we live up to. Liberalism makes God seem so commonplace that He becomes meaningless, while legalism makes God so small that He becomes insignificant.

The negative aspect of a legalistic worldview is that you create what becomes your own Islamic faith. It's really a set of do's and don'ts that allow someone to judge whether others are good people or good Muslims. The problem is, we're always going to create a list we can live up to—which means we're not even living up to the standards of our list, which is a form of self-idolatry. Don't smoke, don't drink, sit and drink water, use your right hand—if you can do all those things, then you redeem yourself—even though your life may be filled with jealousy, greed, lust, and every other deadly vice.

Dealing with situations as a teacher, I became keenly aware of our utter failure as human beings to live up to the pure standard of God. Even the best of people I knew fell hopelessly short, which convinced me even more of the need for grace. I came to understand the importance of the Holy Book—the divine bridge between God and man—without which there is a big gap between us and God. But hearing that and seeing it in people's lives are two different things. Fortunately, God is gracious. And just as He exercises grace toward me, I have to exercise grace toward others. It is easy to want Him to exercise grace toward me; the real reach is becoming anxious for Him to exercise grace toward others.

Today, grace affects everything I think and do. In every decision I make as a head, as a father, as a spouse, as a friend, it has an impact on me. When I think of my teachers, parents, friends, and other important people in my life, I remember both their inspiring encouragement and their eagerness to see me succeed. God gave them to me as examples of how we can grant grace to each other. I pray I never lose sight of the lesson they taught.

> "Once you move your reference point, everything else becomes chaos."

CHAPTER 4

Dare to Teach

Part One

Work hard in silence, let your success be the noise

If you're going through hell—keep going.

—*Winston Churchill*

An owner of the school, who had not previously given the schedule for lesson observation, quietly stepped into the class, and I, as Principal, followed her. Finding a seat in one corner of the class, we both settled down for observation. The story was from *Aladdin*, where Aladdin finds himself trapped in the cave. Aladdin was still wearing a magic ring the sorcerer had lent him. The boys were rapt in the story when the Founder and Director of the School asked the teacher to stop reading. She came in front of the class and asked for the pronunciation of *Aladdin*. The boys pronounced it the way the teacher had done. She was furious, and addressing the English teacher, she expressed her distaste at her pronunciation of *Aladdin*. Then she asked the boys to repeat after her: "ALAIDIN." I was flabbergasted. I was sixty-five years old, and eighty per cent of my life had been spent on the school campus; I had never heard that shade of pronunciation. Later, I looked up the dictionary for pronunciation. It showed thirteen variations of *Aladdin*, but none like hers. Our English teachers had told us that for proper nouns there were no hard and fast rules for pronunciation. Here they were being told to specifically follow what she said. She had no remorse for the teacher who was humiliated in front of the class. The poor teacher sheepishly stood in front of the boys.

In another school the Vice Principal, who had previously given the schedule for lesson observation, quietly stepped into the class with me, as Headmaster of Middle School, following him. Finding a seat in one corner of the class, we both settled down for observation. The story was from Homer's *The Odyssey*, where Odysseus and his men confront the Cyclops. The boys watched a movie clip showing how the clever Greek hero blinded that wine-swilling, man-eating, one-eyed monster and escaped. Giving some instructions to the students, the teacher asked his class to break up into groups and write down various plot points of the story they had just studied. After about ten minutes, he reviewed the points out loud.

The boys loved the blood, bellowing, running around, and sailing away. There was a lot of confusion about who was who and what was going on. In other words, many of the students were having a tough time figuring out the story. So they set to work helping them figure it out. After all, it's hard to understand the significance of a story if you don't understand the story itself.

The Vice Principal, who was observing the lesson with me, later scolded the teacher for "lack of academic rigour". Instead of merely "identifying" what was going on, he believed the teacher should have been working higher up the cognitive food chain by "analysing," "differentiating," and "inferring" everything from motivations to psychological states of the characters.

Yet the Vice Principal knew as well as I did that at least one of these boys could barely read. Ahsan, a fourteen-year-old recent inductee from Dubai, would give bland smiles whenever anyone glanced at him. I had instructed the teacher to give him some fourth-grade reading material and multiple-choice questions about the text to get a basic sense of his reading level. When asked how it was, he replied, "Easy," giving a broad smile. His answers showed he had no idea what the material was. Ahsan produced neat, clean assignments—copied versions of what was presented on the whiteboard.

All other teachers had the same experience with Ahsan, and the Vice Principal told them to get together and figure out how to bring him up to speed in their "spare time." Whenever there was an issue with a student who was far behind or had behavioural problems, they were told to handle the situation in their spare time. Unfortunately, with his good behaviour and smiling demeanour, Ahsan was often given extra time by teachers occupied with other problems.

The Vice Principal also knew that some students had other obvious special needs and learning disabilities which were largely ignored or undiagnosed. One student, Omar, spent most of the forty-five-minute period punching the students around him and poking fingers at them. Bigger and taller than the other boys, Omar was a lovable bear of a kid. He had a serious case of attention deficit hyperactivity disorder (ADHD). When he entered the class at the end of the day, his school uniform was blotched with sweat, ink, and the remains of major and minor food fights throughout the day. His shirttails were out, and his tie was loose and flapping like a pennant carried by the colour guard of a battle-weary regiment.

Despite seven previous periods of punching, throwing, running, shouting, backpack-swinging, and desk-pounding, by the time he joined the class for eighth period, Omar was still raring to go. If another kid wasn't goading him by stealing his backpack and stuffing it in the trash can, or challenging him for a contest ("Omar, you go first"), he had his neck craned as he searched the classroom for some action, the way an English pointer searches for a pheasant.

Omar was among the students with obvious special-education needs. There were a number of other kids like him who needed special help. But dealing with these students as the law required would have meant employing special-education teachers. Not only are qualified special-education teachers in short supply, but the low student-teacher ratio required by the rules would eat up the school's budget. So instead of directly addressing the problems of these kids, the administration made the students' problems the classroom teachers' problem, pretending they weren't really special-education students at all.

The Vice Principal also knew that Aamir was far ahead of the rest of the class. When Aamir discovered that the class was going to cover *The Odyssey*, he read all he could find on the topic in the class textbook and online. Aamir was tall and thin, and wore thick glasses. Bright, eager, and ready with the correct answer to every question ever asked, Aamir was the perfect student.

Although Aamir was ready for an in-depth discussion of *The Odyssey*, most of the rest of the class were still trying to figure out what the Greeks were doing in the Cyclops' cave, or silently taunting kids across the room: "Nerd."

But teachers dared not challenge the Vice Principal's assessment. Some had done that before and been shot down. Trying to get some help for Ahsan's ADHD (which would benefit not only him, but also his classmates and teachers) simply led to the Vice Principal's suggestion that Ahsan was acting out because teachers weren't sufficiently challenging "the writer within him."

"Oh no. He is a very good student," the Vice Principal assured them, waving the issue away with a flutter of his hand. The Principal and Vice Principal were quite clear that the school was a model school, and teachers quickly realised they were to enforce that idea. As they saw it, all low student achievement and wildly inappropriate behaviour would be overcome by enforcing the Principal's vision statements, expectations, non-negotiables, and various other big ideas.

If pressed about Ahsan's inability to read, teachers would be told that if they were good teachers, they would spend as much time as necessary with him to improve his skills. If raised again, they would be told
that if they were good teachers, they would be able to "engage" him with interesting work or use "the force of their personality" to make him—and the other twenty-seven boys—sit quietly for the forty-five-minute lesson.

And if Aamir's issue was raised—that he was so far ahead of the class that it wasn't fair to keep him there—teachers were told that if they were good teachers, every lesson should span the wide range of academic skills among the students. In other words, each lesson every day should be tailored to each of their 120 students' individual needs—targeting every gradation between illiterate and near-college—and revised constantly. Something that was next to impossible. Teachers were busy teaching from early morning till late night.

After putting in forty years of teaching and serving as head of schools, I came upon a chain system with more than two hundred branches in the country. My job was to observe not only the teachers but the heads of schools.

Little did I know I was entering a system where all teachers were considered bad until proven otherwise.

From what I saw, each school's principal had so much leeway that good management and honest evaluation were easily crushed under the weight of Crazy Boss Syndrome. In my experience, the much-boasted "data" and other measurements of student progress and teacher ability were far more random and manipulated than parents had been led to believe.

The heads would often harp, "Discipline and classroom management will be taken care of by how we talk."

"Frame everything in a positive way," they were told. "Don't say 'don't.'"

If a student is running in the hall, don't say, "Don't run." Say, "Please walk."

Plus, individual teachers had to handle all discipline problems in the classroom. Whether it required talking with parents or sitting with miscreants, it was up to the teacher to keep all students quiet and on task at all times

Teachers were told: "Controlled chaos is not acceptable." They were expected to command the room with sheer composure and unwavering authority, as though personality alone could override structural flaws, behavioural challenges, and systemic negligence. "Use the force of your personality," they said, as if teachers were magicians capable of bending adolescent impulses by charisma alone. It was an unreasonable, almost cruel expectation—one that betrayed how profoundly detached the leadership was from the real conditions inside a classroom.

The following day, an eighth-grade teacher, desperate to comply with these directives, attempted to exercise this so-called "force of personality." He warned the boys repeatedly that unless they quietened down, he would hold them after school. Predictably, this tactic failed—not because the teacher was incompetent, but because no amount of "personality" can override a chaotic environment, undefined boundaries, or inconsistent administrative support. As the school day ended, he stationed himself at the door, weary yet determined.

"No one is leaving," he announced. "You're all staying after school for half an hour."

Ten minutes into this impromptu detention, the Headmistress burst through the door, her expression a mixture of shock and theatrical indignation. "What is going on here?" she demanded. The boys immediately erupted into a frenzy of explanations, each more animated than the last. The teacher, already emotionally exhausted, stood there realising how quickly his authority had been undermined. His attempt to enforce order—an attempt made only because he had been instructed to—

now made him look inept. The Headmistress's reaction signalled to the boys that discipline was negotiable, and worse, that a teacher's authority was fragile and disposable.

When this teacher sought guidance from a trainer, hoping for clearer boundaries or practical strategies, he was given the same dismissive response: "Oh, you can't hold them all for detention." The implication was unmistakable—teachers were simultaneously expected to maintain discipline yet denied every practical tool to do so. As months went by, the teacher's file filled with criticisms, each one documenting "failure to become a less-bad teacher," a phrase that said more about the system's dysfunction than about his abilities. The goal was never improvement—it was evidence building.

In truth, it became increasingly clear that the Headmistress was not interested in moulding him into a strong, confident educator. Her objective was far simpler: to prove that he was a bad teacher. A convenient scapegoat absolved the system of introspection. His struggles allowed them to reaffirm their favourite illusion —that the school was a "model institution," and that any cracks in its façade existed only because of flawed teachers.

But beneath the surface, everyone knew the truth. Teachers were terrified to express dissent openly, for dissent meant punishment. Many confided in whispers, in corridors, or behind closed doors—but silence reigned in official meetings. They had seen what happened to those who questioned unrealistic expectations or challenged unjust policies. Files were built, reputations eroded, and careers dismantled with clinical precision.

The tragedy was that good teachers—dedicated, thoughtful educators—were being suffocated by a leadership model that prized obedience over professionalism, appearances over substance, and compliance over truth. And the children paid the heaviest price. For when a school strips teachers of dignity, autonomy, and respect, it strips students of genuine learning. The classroom becomes merely a stage where adults pretend to teach and children pretend to learn, all while the system congratulates itself on hollow achievements.

This is the silent suffering of many schools: where the loudest voices are those who have never taught, the strictest judgments come from those who have never managed a classroom, and the grandest visions are built by those who refuse to step into the chaos they insist on controlling. And in the midst of it all, the teachers continue—tired, overstretched, but still hoping that one day the system will value truth over theatrics, and education over ego.

-End of Part 1-

Dare to Teach

Part Two

When Teachers Fall, Schools Crumble: A Story of Disrespect and Resilience

The Exiled Educator: How Schools Are Punishing the Very People Who Build Them

---

A number of good teachers left the school for better prospects. The new schools were ready to give them handsome salaries, and their administrations understood that by catching these "big fish" they would secure a surge of students. They were successful in that mission. These teachers were not only good; they were the very people who had helped establish these institutions. The school they left behind saw its discipline deteriorate, and its results began to decline steadily. The contrast became painfully visible as the vacuum created by the loss of experienced teachers began to widen.

But those were the days when teachers were still given a show-cause notice, at the very least, to defend themselves and prove their innocence. Now the principal arrives with a heavy hand, and teachers who have served twenty to thirty years are handed a termination letter first thing in the morning when they arrive at school. To humiliate them further, the letter is delivered by the security guards. The administration gives them no chance to speak, no room to justify themselves, and no opportunity to explain years of dedicated work. Teachers who have served a school for so long are honoured elsewhere—other schools celebrate them, recognise them, and cherish their contribution. But this school, instead of honouring its teachers, chooses to discard them as if they were a burden.

The only teacher who has ever been honoured was an Englishman. The English abhorrence of foreign habits is well known. When they are obliged to live abroad for years, they refuse either to accustom themselves to foreign food or to learn foreign languages. According to George Orwell, nearly every Englishman considers it effeminate to pronounce a foreign word correctly. Meanwhile, we have been labelled— in Churchill's unforgettable words— as "semi-apes who should be reduced quite openly to slavery," people who could interbreed with gorillas. The historical irony is hard to miss, especially when the only celebrated teacher is one who fits neatly into the colonial mindset still lingering unconsciously within certain minds.

The callousness truly began with the arrival of the new principal, who had neither understanding nor sympathy for the local teachers and their cultural sensibilities. No homework is done beforehand; knee-jerk reactions and jumping to conclusions have become the order of the day. Those who refuse to conform are kept in a state of slavish subjugation, intimidated into silence. This often happens right in the middle of the academic session. Students suffer, classes suffer, and teachers endure humiliation at the hands of the very guards hired to protect the environment of the institution.

Arm-twisting and pressurising teachers to change loyalties results in splintering the staff and fracturing the unity that once existed. Consequently, pygmies are selected, nurtured, promoted, and brought into prominence—with entirely predictable results. It resembles NAB's selective accountability, which, instead of deterring, simply goes dormant and awakens at a convenient moment. The message it sends is completely wrong: yielding to pressure becomes the only way to survive, and choosing the wrong policy becomes "right" as long as it pleases the powers controlling the narrative.

The unfair treatment by the school administration eventually created a complete market for teachers. Many of them set up their own tuition centres, and these centres prospered; in a strange twist of fate, some even felt grateful to the school for taking action against them. One teacher joked that if he had not been asked to leave, he would never have owned a house of his own. Their parent institution, however, suffered badly. Far more serious academic work was now taking place in the evening academies. The institutions they left behind began to face worsening discipline problems, and yet, instead of recognising the chain reaction they themselves created, the administration chose to blame the new set of teachers for everything that went wrong.

With so many capable teachers forced out and replaced by mediocre or below-average ones, the students naturally became more disruptive and were allowed to rob their classmates of precious teaching time.

Break time turned into a horrendous experience; bloody fights became routine, and chaos was no longer shocking. When the principal was apprised of the increasingly dangerous situation, he advised the person to keep it private— and insisted the matter must not be given any further air. The general feeling among everyone was that the head, a ruthless roughneck supported by an insensitive board, had arrived to prove everybody wrong. More teachers would be thrown out unless they became compliant lackeys. Fear and uncertainty became the new normal.

The school environment no longer suited the more sensitive boys—which, in truth, meant most of them: ordinary boys with ordinary human weaknesses. Many had already had their spirits broken in boarding houses, and while such places may suit a hot-tempered or aggressive youth, they are never right for someone tender, thoughtful, or naturally docile. The harshness does not shape them; it quietly crushes them from within.

The school also lacks a genuine intellectual drive. Its focus seems more on producing wealth than cultivating learning. Many boys have become dependent, passive, and timid when facing new challenges. Their timidity often hides behind bravado, bursts of anger, or aggression, yet beneath this noise lies a deep emptiness—a lack of inner strength. Much of this stems from seeing teachers publicly humiliated. I heard of one incident where the principal barged into a classroom, stopped the lesson, and ordered the boys to tear out a page of their work, crush it, and throw it at the whiteboard. Turning to the head of department, he declared the teacher unfit to teach.

This humiliating behaviour deeply embarrassed the teacher and encouraged students to misbehave even more. Knowing nothing would happen to them, discipline fell to an unprecedented low. Matters became so serious that security guards were stationed around the academic block as bouncers—to control boys, intimidate teachers, and report directly to the principal. Such scenes are unheard of in Pakistan. Yes, they may occur in America or England, but never here, and never with this level of indignity.

When I began my career, I asked one of my senior colleagues, "Dozens and dozens of teenagers scrutinise my language, clothing, and posture all day long, all week long. If it happens to be my bad day, what exactly do I do?" His cynical smile widened before he replied, "The students will tell you. They'll comment on your taste in neckties, your hairstyle, and the quality of your lessons. All of us teachers are evaluated every single day, all day long already. It's one of the most exhausting aspects of our job." He rattled all this off in quick succession, and before he left, he added one last piece of advice—"Don't adopt teaching as a career."

His response left me dazed for a while, but eventually it became an eye-opener. As a new teacher I laughed it off, not fully understanding that teaching is, and always has been, a high-pressure job. The truth is, teachers don't actually need anyone to tell them when they are doing poorly or when something is going wrong—our students tell us directly and indirectly. When they are not learning, they signal it loudly. They put their heads down table, or they pass notes across the room. They raise their hands repeatedly for clarification. And sometimes, they simply stare at us blankly, like zombies. Few things are more excruciating for a teacher than leading a classroom where the learning is not happening and where every moment feels like a silent indictment.

Teaching is never like other jobs. In most professions, when you work, no one is deliberately interrupting you. But in teaching, there is always something—a child disrupting the lesson, another searching for a pencil, an office boy knocking, the principal calling for report-card evidence, or messages asking about "signs of improvement." Slowly, a teacher develops an edginess that never existed before entering the profession.

A teacher must have thick skin. The job is extremely demanding, especially now with budget cuts and constant changes in special-education policies. Class sizes have increased, support staff have been removed, and students with serious learning needs are pushed into mainstream classrooms, where they struggle with a curriculum driven by high-stakes testing. The strain, as always, falls on the teacher.

When I assign daily homework, it becomes 240 sheets by week's end. Giving each even a few minutes would mean countless hours of correction, not including preparation, which should take twice as long. Teachers also shoulder leadership roles: some run the School Model UN, others the student council, magazines, Urdu and English drama—an overwhelming load. I once heard my son tell his mother tearfully, "I am not good at anything." At that same time, I was teaching advanced classes full of students praised as "good at everything," receiving letters and visits from parents and colleges thanking me for my efforts. I was a good teacher—but was I a good father? If teaching was my greatest strength, didn't my own child deserve more of it?

Super Hero Principals

We must stop believing in superhero principals and administrators as the quick and easy solution to this problem. They are myths, products of popular imagination. 'Visionary managers' are not going to save our students and schools. In fact, from what I've seen, the opposite is true. In today's educational system, not only does power corrupt, but combining power and data corrupts both the person and the data. And that leaves us worse off than ever.

Campaigns for school reform and corporate-style management of our public schools are sweeping the country. As a result, individual principals have been given a stunning amount of power and leeway to decide who is a good teacher and who is a bad teacher. With that much authority in the hands of a few top administrators, who have little accountability for their decisions, it becomes easy for good management and honest evaluations of teachers to be trampled during administrators' attempts to deliver stellar results in unrealistically short periods of time.

Schools are misguiding the board. The school board is naïve but pompous by virtue of their position in society. The school meetings with the principal produce nothing but the prison of his thoughts. The meetings are a special kind of torture. Teachers are prisoners of the "Yes, sir!" syndrome, even though they are told they may argue. Although these are educated, intelligent people, they almost always stay quiet or agree with the principal. That is why, when you observe classes, you will hardly find students asking questions. One of the reasons we do not produce inquiring minds.

Governing Body

We are prisoners of a paternalistic approach. This has been observed in the meetings of the Governing Body, where the senior-most member dictates his terms. Individuality is crushed even in meetings of such a high level, where the Governor of a province is in the chair. Bad decisions emanate from gatherings of this stature. Imagine some generals, big businessmen, and old boys of high position masquerading as educationists, presenting themselves as souls of purity and models of scrupulous honesty, their only qualification being that they once studied in the school for some years.

Most of the members are former students of the school who now hold high positions. Some of these members are young and have a clear conflict of interest, as their sons are studying in the school, while their grandsons are bona fide students as well. Holding cabinet positions means many of these members will hardly find time for the meetings. The question that comes to mind is this: yes, they were old students, but does that mean the school must remain at a standstill and endlessly talk nostalgically about how things were in their time? The contract between their parents and the school administration expired long ago. Their parents paid the fee, they received their education, and since then education has moved forward.

Moreover, most of them are politicians. Just wait five minutes and the Minister of Education will suddenly become the Minister for Roads.

Why do we consider laying off people within our organisation? If someone has a job, they should not be fired for performance issues. If they struggle, they should be coached and supported—just as we would support a child who brings home a 'D' from school. This is why so many people feel deep anger towards banking CEOs with their disproportionate salaries and bonuses. They violate a social contract by allowing their own people to be sacrificed to protect their interests—or worse, sacrificing them deliberately. That is what offends us, not the numbers themselves. Would anyone object if we gave one hundred and fifty million dollars to Edhi? Or a two-hundred-and-fifty-million-dollar bonus to Mother Teresa? No—none at all.

We call true leaders the ones who sacrifice for their people so they may feel safe, protected, and able to prosper. People will give their blood, sweat, and tears to fulfil such a leader's vision.

The real problem is that, with so many issues in the educational system, blaming teachers is easier than fixing the system itself. This has handed many public schools to "visionary managers" who believe strict procedures and data-driven business principles will somehow reform Pakistani education.

The Governing Body must conduct a proper survey for the principal's appraisal. All other workers in the school undergo appraisal, so why should the head of the institution be above the law? A Governing Body member should lead a full presentation and discussion on principal mistreatment.

The board, in its position, is legally, professionally, and ethically responsible for the general welfare and safety of teachers, for overseeing the conduct of school administrators, and for protecting and providing relief for victims of mistreatment. Without protective policies and procedures, teachers who are subjected to mistreatment by school principals have little recourse. The role of the board is especially important in light of research on workplace abuse, which shows that upper-level management in organisations often ignores or colludes with abusive bosses when victims make formal complaints. Moreover, they may inadvertently contribute to the problem through the attitudes they convey about teachers and the expectations they hold for school-level administrators.

The teachers deserve the best, and they also deserve to be part of major decisions that affect the classroom and the children. If a majority of teachers do not like a curriculum or programme that the administration is in love with, then that programme should not be used. Teaching is physically gruelling and emotionally demanding work; it requires a great commitment of time and self. The motivation to teach comes from love and money; and odd and unexpected gifts, along with more than a little courage, can make an ordinary person an extraordinary teacher.

Imagine a school with more than 250 teachers and one really bad principal, and he thinks most of the teachers do not know what they are doing, so he tells them what to do— and that advice backfires. Who do you think gets blamed for that principal's failure? There were clear signs that the school board is selected, and sometimes some can be misguided and ignorant, and it does not help when the principal is just as bad or worse. The school system is bureaucratic, frustrating, and constantly hindered by forces, vested interests, and power struggles. The size of the board guarantees frustration, alienation, and burnout.

The way the school is governed needs a drastic overhaul. We need dreamers.

I hope that our society will come to reward our teachers in a manner that will make them as independent as other people—not rich over night, but able to save a few rupees before retirement, to have enough money to send the kids to trips, to buy a few things extra for their wife—and yes, maybe make it possible for papa to join a club before he is sixty. But this is possible only when feudal lords begin to show respect for teachers.

Tailpiece

It is fascinating to note that schools and schooling are becoming increasingly irrelevant to the great enterprises of the planet. No one truly believes anymore that scientists are trained in science classes, or politicians in civics classes, or poets in English classes. The truth is that schools do not really teach anything except how to obey orders. Although teachers genuinely care and work very, very hard, the institution itself is psychopathic—it has no conscience. A bell rings, and the young man in the middle of writing a poem must close his notebook and move to a different cell, where he must memorise that humans and monkeys derive from a common ancestor.

Here is a curious idea to ponder: Senator Ted Kennedy's office released a paper claiming that prior to compulsory education, the state literacy rate was ninety-eight per cent, and that after it was introduced the figure never exceeded ninety-one per cent, where it stood in 1990. Here is another curiosity to consider: the home-schooling movement has quietly grown to the point where one and a half million young people are being educated entirely by their own parents. Last month the education press reported the remarkable news that, in their ability to think, children schooled at home seem to be five or even ten years ahead of their formally trained peers.

Out of the 168 hours in each week, children sleep 56 hours. That leaves 112 hours in which to fashion a self. According to recent reports, children watch 55 hours of television a week. That then leaves them 57 hours in which to grow up. Children attend school for 30 hours a week, spend about eight hours getting ready for and travelling to and from school, and devote an average of seven hours a week to homework—a total of 45 hours. During that time, they are under constant surveillance. They have no private time or private space and are disciplined if they try to assert individuality in the use of either.

That leaves them 12 hours a week from which to create a unique consciousness. Children must eat, too, and that takes some time—not much, because they have largely lost the tradition of family dining—but if we allot three hours a week to evening meals, we arrive at a net amount of private time for each child of nine hours per week.

"Little did I know I was entering a system where all teachers were considered bad until proven otherwise."

CHAPTER 5

Why Science and Not Arts

Why I Chose Arts: Embracing Empathy, Imagination, and Moral Growth

---

The Value of Arts in a Science-Driven World

Education has been the central motif of my life. I was sent to a boarding school where, you could say, I grew up. Education in our home was almost a moral value. According to my father, my schooling at one of the best schools in Pakistan should be a launching pad from which I could leap into my full potential. It was not easy for me to settle into a posh school environment that felt completely alien. I was coming from an inner-city area where low places were choked drains, inundation, and heaps of unremoved refuse. "You have to survive," my father said, in order to succeed in life. I had no idea what that meant, but he held the reins firmly in his hands, and one simply had to succumb to his will. My mother, being a typical domestic mother who had dedicated her life to her family, never questioned him and quietly agreed.

My father was a meticulous file keeper. After I graduated from Lawrence College, he showed me my personal file—a revelation of my life. At a cursory glance I noticed the word "money." All my letters from junior school to senior school demanded money. I quickly went through different letters and, to my amazement, they all asked for money. I became curious to know more. The letters were full of mistakes corrected by him. He was very keen that I should become fluent in writing. These letters were often sent back to me with instructions to post them to him again after making the necessary corrections. I learned to spell "receive," to understand "the rule for double past tense," "subject-verb agreement," the difference between "quite" and "quiet," and perhaps even their difference in pronunciation. There were many more lessons, though my memory fades.

He was also particular about sending me Sports Times, a sports magazine, every month. Knowing my interest in sports, he believed the magazine would serve two purposes: I would read it with interest, and it would expose me to English while adding to my knowledge of sports.

His intention was to make me apt in the language of power. But unknowingly he had instilled in me, and sensitised me to, the finer elements of life. I developed a habit of reading. Assisted by my teachers, I began to read a great many immortal works: Jack the Giant-Killer, Jack and the Beanstalk, The Yellow Dwarf, Sindbad the Sailor, Beauty and the Beast, Aladdin and the Wonderful Lamp, along with several others of a similar character. From my rudimental books—books that truly deserved the name because they blended so well with the rudimental mind—I passed on, without being conscious of any break or division, to books on which the learned are content to write commentaries and dissertations, but which I found to be just as pleasant children's books as any of the others. Old Homer wrote admirably for little folk, especially in the Odyssey.

We were still in Junior School when the boys in our dormitory decided to buy Junior Classics comics. We used to walk every month to the Mall in Murree and were given Rs 5 to spend. Each of us bought one comic that cost 8 annas, and the rest of the money was spent on toffees and drinking Vimto or Fanta. With this background, I intuitively preferred to opt for the arts and not science.

Opting for Arts

Science subjects were a Herculean task for me—no, they were simply not for me. But in Pakistan it was, and still is, a fashion to become a doctor or an engineer; there was, apparently, no other respectable job to do. I, too, was expected to take science subjects. All my cousins had their heads down, determined to achieve the ultimate. Studying arts was considered the choice of those who did not do well. I was fortunate to be in the boarding house, so I quietly switched over to arts.

It is a great disservice to students to devalue the arts, which I believe results from thinking of knowledge in a very narrow, utilitarian way. I was often asked the same questions by family elders: Why would you take arts? Why would you study poetry? What will you ever do with poetry? Poetry was obviously not a practical skill, because it did not teach you how to build an electric circuit or conduct an experiment in osmosis. But poetry and the arts are practical—if we widen our definition of practical.

They develop the ability to think, to empathise, to imagine.

I would much rather have a physician who reads literature, because such a person is more likely to know that a human being must be understood as a whole—emotionally, mentally, spiritually—and not merely as a logical collection of bones and flesh. When my daughter said she wanted to be a doctor, my spontaneous answer was: "Wear the white coat with dignity and pride; it is an honour and privilege to serve the public as a physician." And I added: learn to be a good human being—never become materialistic.

Moral Growth

I feel it is the duty of our elders to teach the notion that all moral growth consists of growing from self to others. They understand from experience that children say, "What can you do for me?" or "What is the country giving me?" but adults say, "What can I do for you?" They readily accept the idea that we do not grow up when we can take care of ourselves; rather, we truly grow up only when we can take care of others—and want to. By merely insisting that we become doctors or engineers, our parents were hinting at the ambitious pursuit of things: fashionable clothes and cars, trendy expensive gadgets, a hefty portfolio. This sort of consumerist lust is only part of the problem. After all, as we have all experienced, many well-off people can possess all sorts of things without being materialistic

Materialism really means seeing and treating other

people as things. It considers man (in the philosophical sense) as merely an object—a clever beast. This is where the evil lies.

I understand the good intentions behind the idea of keeping everyone comfortable, which is particularly an American ideal, but I think it is important to make peace with discomfort. There is something perverse about expecting always to be comfortable. Life is messy; sometimes discomfort opens us to growth, knowledge, and meaning. It is especially relevant today, in a country with deep political divisions. I believe it is impossible to engage honestly without some discomfort. Do not choose comfort over truth. Do not run away from reality.

> *"Don't choose comfort over truth. Don't run away from reality."*

CHAPTER 6

The Power to Imagine Better

A Teacher's Journey Through Failure, Reflection, and Transformation

One who often reflects,
Develops his foresight.

HAZRAT ALI (A.S)

I was in the middle of a lesson when a sudden noise diverted my attention: a desk had been pushed away and struck the boy sitting in front. The next boy reacted equally disturbingly, and suddenly there was a chain reaction, as may happen in any ordinary class. I grew concerned; nothing of this sort had ever happened in my class.
The first boy responded, "A lizard fell on my desk, sir." I was relieved, chortled with delight, and then smirked at

the boy. I tried to control the situation by talking to the class about how my generation had failed to get Kashmir. I had just begun when, from the corner of my eye, I spied the flustered lizard creeping up the raised platform of the teacher. My voice changed; still trying to keep my composure, I continued with my story.

I did not have to continue for long. A boy sitting at the end of the class came crawling forward and pounced at the lizard. He caught it and started patting it. I looked at him, perturbed, and the class too became curious. He brought the creature close to me to pat it. I withdrew myself, though he kept convincing me that it would not say anything. The boy was a gentle human being. Without much persuasion, he went out into the corridor, gently put the lizard down, and came back in. He quietly returned to his seat. I heaved a huge sigh of relief. The class was now waiting for my reaction.

My mind was swirling, searching for a way to assign meaning to the episode. I knew that split-second decision-making is a crucial aspect of teaching. I was thinking on my feet and came up with a solution. I had often called myself a drifter. I had not cared much about covering the curriculum, and this was where the pressure came. I had often faced the wrath of the administration and parents, who felt that I should not be doing things differently. I had received subtle and overt messages that I needed to pay more attention to covering the curriculum and that I should find a more equal balance between process and product.

When I regained my composure, I called Salman, the reptile hobbyist, to explain how he was able to do such an extraordinary thing so confidently. We came to know that Salman had an avid interest in herpetology. At home, he kept lizards and snakes in glass cages. He was confident hat they do not do anything to human beings unless they are provoked. I requested him to bring his glass cages to class the next day, and I took the responsibility of obtaining permission from the Headmaster.

The next day was a happening one. We had a long discussion on reptiles, and I seized the opportunity to give them an assignment on the topic. They were given two weeks to complete it. Two weeks later, I received some of the most pleasing work.

The life force of teaching practice is thinking and wondering. We carry home those moments of the day that touch us, and we question the decisions we made. During these times of reflection, we realise when something needs to change. Often, it is only through reflection that we even recognise that we had a choice—that we could have done something differently.

Life Changing Experience (Teaching)

When I look back at life, I realise it was never a bed of roses. I had failed on an epic scale according to my family and relatives, and by every usual measure of failure I was the greatest failure, for I had become a teacher. I knew that period of my life was a dark one. I had not become a doctor or an engineer. I had no idea then how far the tunnel extended, and for a long time any light at the end of it was a hope rather than a reality.

I stopped pretending to myself that I was anything other than what I was, and began directing all my energy into teaching—the only work that mattered to me, where I truly belonged. I promised myself that I would be different from other teachers. I was set free because my greatest fear had been realised and I was still alive. Rock bottom became the solid foundation on which I rebuilt my life. You might never fail on the scale that I did, but some failure in life is inevitable. It is impossible to live without failing at something, unless you live so cautiously that you might as well not have lived at all—in which case, you fail by default.

I started my teaching career against all odds. My father and family did not have the heart to approve of teaching as a career. They could not think beyond becoming a doctor or an engineer. I would like to make it clear, in parenthesis, that I do not blame my parents for that point of view. There is an expiry date on blaming one's parents for steering one in the wrong direction; the moment you are old enough to take the wheel of life in your own hands, responsibility lies with you. Moreover, I cannot criticise my parents for hoping that I would never experience poverty. They had been poor themselves, and I have since been poor, and I quite agree with them that it is not an ennobling experience. Poverty entails fear and stress and sometimes depression; it means a thousand petty humiliations and hardships. Climbing out of poverty by your own efforts is something on which to pride yourself, but poverty itself is romanticised only by fools.

What I feared most for myself when I was young was not poverty, but failure. Despite a distinct lack of motivation at university—where I had spent far too much time enjoying myself and far too little time listening to lectures—I had a knack for passing examinations. For years, that had been a measure of success in my life and in the lives of my peers. I had hardly known heartbreak, hardship, or heartache.

I do not for a moment suppose that all my friends and I enjoyed an existence of unruffled privilege and contentment; however, the fact that I graduated from

Lawrence College suggests that I was not very well acquainted with failure. One may be driven by the fear of failure just as much as by the desire for success. Indeed, our conception of failure might not be too far removed from the average person's idea of success—so high have we flown already in simply being students of Lawrence College.

Ultimately, we all have to decide for ourselves what constitutes failure, but the world is quite eager to give us its own set of criteria if we let it.

Failure gave me an inner security that I had never attained by passing examinations. It taught me things about myself that I could have learned in no other way. I discovered that I had a strong will, and more discipline than I had suspected. I also found out that I had friends whose value was truly above the price of rubies. The knowledge that you have emerged wiser and stronger from setbacks means that you are ever after secure in your ability to survive.

You will never truly know the strength of your relationships until both parties have been tested by adversity. Such knowledge is a true gift—painfully won—and it has been worth more to me than any qualification I ever earned.

Given a Time-Turner, I would tell my 21-year-old self that personal happiness lies in knowing that life is not a checklist of acquisition or achievement. Your qualifications and your CV are not your life, though you will meet many people of my age and older who confuse the two. Life is difficult and complicated and beyond anyone's total control, and the humility to know that will enable you to survive its vicissitudes.

Importance of Imagination

You might think I chose the importance of imagination for the part it played in rebuilding my life. But that is not wholly so, though I will personally defend the value of bedtime stories to my last gasp. I have learned to value imagination in a much broader sense. Imagination is the unique human capacity to envision—that is the beginning of all invention. It is arguably its most transformative and revelatory capacity. It is the power that enables us to empathise with human beings whose experiences we have never shared.

One of the greatest formative experiences of my life preceded my entry into teaching; this revelation came through my life experiences. Every day, I saw more evidence of the evils humankind can inflict on their fellow humans in order to gain or maintain power. I began to have nightmares—literal nightmares—about some of the things I saw, heard, and read. And yet, I also learned more about human goodness.

The power of human empathy, leading to collective action, saves lives and frees prisoners. Ordinary people, whose personal well-being and security are assured, join together in vast numbers to save people they do not know and will never meet. Unlike any other creature on this planet, human beings can learn and understand without having experienced; they can think themselves into other people's places.

Many prefer not to exercise their imagination at all. They choose to remain comfortably within the bounds of their own experience, never troubling themselves to wonder how it would feel to have been born other than they are. They can refuse to hear screams or peer inside cages. They can close their minds to any suffering that does not touch them personally. They can refuse to know. I might be tempted to envy people who can live that way —except that I do not think they have any fewer nightmares than I do.

I believe the wilfully unimaginative see more monsters. They are often more afraid. What is more, those who choose not to empathise enable monsters, for without ever committing an act of outright evil themselves, they connive with it through their own apathy.

Plutarch said that what we achieve inwardly will change outer reality. That is an astonishing statement, and yet it is proven a thousand times every day of our lives. It expresses, in part, our inescapable connection with the outside world—the fact that we touch other people's lives simply by existing.

If you choose to use your status and influence to raise your voice on behalf of those who have no voice—if you choose to identify not only with the powerful, but with the powerless; if you retain the ability to imagine yourself into the lives of those who do not have your advantages— then it will not only be your proud families who celebrate your existence, but thousands and millions of people whose reality you have changed.

We do not need magic to transform our world. We carry all the power we need inside ourselves already. We have the power to imagine better.

We do not need magic to transform the world—only the courage to imagine better.

CHAPTER 7
Reading
Culture, and the Struggle for Identity

Reflections on Language, Literature, and Postcolonial Education

A reader lives a thousand lives before he dies. The man who never reads, lives only once.

Richard Martin

My school friend, Athar Tahir, a poet, author, translator, painter, a 1974 Rhodes Scholar at Oxford, a 1984 Hubert Humphrey Fellow, and a recipient of the Patras Bokhari Award—has had an illustrious career. His poems have been set as texts for secondary schools and for the "O" Levels, University of Cambridge, and have been included in several Oxford University Press and other anthologies. They have also been translated into Urdu, Chinese, and Italian. His books on literature, art, and culture have won eleven national and international awards. He has been awarded the Tamgha-i-Imtiaz (1998) and the Sitara-i-Imtiaz (2009) for his contributions.

He sent me a clip from the movie Detachment (2011) on WhatsApp—a very pertinent piece, one that made me think. I immediately watched the entire movie on YouTube. It is a sort of emotional horror film for educators. It sparked my imagination and brought back memories of forty years of teaching. I would like to quote from the movie before delving deeper into what I had been thinking as a teacher:

"How are you to imagine anything if the images are always provided for you? To deliberately believe in lies while knowing that they are false—for example, I need to be pretty to be happy; I need surgery to be pretty; I need to be thin, famous, fashionable. This is a marketing holocaust twenty-four hours a day for the rest of your lives. The powers that be are hard at work dumbing us to death. So, to defend ourselves and fight against assimilating this dullness into our thought processes, we must learn to read —

to stimulate our own imagination,
to cultivate our own consciousness,
and our own belief systems.

We all need these skills to defend and preserve our own minds."

For me, the last sentence was the most striking: **"We must learn to read."**

He emphasised stimulating our own imagination, cultivating our own consciousness, and forming our own belief systems. That triggered a thought process.

We, as parents, encourage our children to read—but read what?

It has now been deeply ingrained in our children's

minds that they must read. Some children pick up books at random; others get help from teachers; others seek recommendations from friends. All kinds of literature are available in the market. Children need guidance. Invariably, many pick books that alienate them from their culture, because the books they read are written in an alien language; from that language emanates an alien culture, alien imagination—imported imagination—that does not help in original thinking.
So how does reading affect your history, your culture, and the knowledge carried by your language?

Reading is the bedrock of education. I believe there is something wonderful and affirming about reading—and particularly about reading what is familiar, what reflects your own self in fiction and literature. I have no doubt that the greatest gift a parent can give to a child's schooling and future prospects is the ability to read well before starting formal school. It is a parental gift, because the best route to a lifelong intimacy with reading is regular reading sessions that involve both parent and child.

But what **kind of stories** should be read?

Parents must ensure that the stories of their own culture are firmly embedded in their children's minds. Children imbibe the significance of their culture—and the joy of reading—most naturally from their parents. That particular pleasure should never be denied to anyone.
In the past many centuries, white Europeans detonated a "cultural bomb" across the world, diminishing the value of non-white peoples and their ways through colonisation, imperialism, industrialisation, and globalisation.

The effect of this cultural bomb is to annihilate a people's belief in:
- their names,
- their languages,
- their environment,
- their heritage of struggle,
- their unity,
- their capacities,
- and ultimately **in themselves**.

It makes them view their past as a wasteland of non-achievement, prompting them to distance themselves from that "wasteland." It pushes them to identify with what is furthest removed from their own identity—for instance, with the languages of other peoples rather than their own. It makes them identify with what is decadent and reactionary—forces that suppress their own springs of life. It plants doubts about the moral righteousness of struggle. It renders the possibility of triumph or victory as remote, even ridiculous. Its intended results are despair, despondency, and a collective death-wish.

We in the subcontinent lost the capacity to imagine different futures:
—the capacity to picture a different world,
—the capacity to envision different possibilities.

This loss occurred because we were suppressed by our colonisers. Hence, reading our own literature becomes all the more important. But authoritarian regimes, too, have always wanted to limit the capacity to imagine different futures—not only through literature, but through all forms of art, because art has the power to fire the imagination and reveal the realities of the present, even when those realities are unacceptable.

Therefore, if you want to understand the world of today, the literature you must read is the literature of your own country, because it captures reality and helps you begin imagining different possibilities.

But it is equally important to read about people who are not like you—if for no other reason than the simple reality that the world is not full of people like you.

This became particularly evident to me in American bookstores, where I wished it had been considered equally important to offer children's books in which the characters were diverse: white children, black children, brown children, Asian children, Hispanic children—children who are different in all kinds of ways.

If you read diverse books to your children, you prepare them—hopefully—for a world in which their conception of people is wider and healthier. But this should only come after the child is well-versed in his own culture.

I do not merely want my children to read about people who do not look like me. Yet this is precisely what happens in Pakistan. Children are exposed to American or European stories in which black is bad and white is good, where a duckling is "bad" simply for being black, where Snow White is an angel, where whiteness symbolises beauty and blackness symbolises ugliness. Our children read these books, absorb the contents of an alien culture, and begin to accept such ideas unconsciously.

Since parents often fail to monitor their children's reading choices, children become exposed to all kinds of trash literature. Teenagers are encouraged to develop a reading habit; parents are pleased to see their children reading, but rarely bother to check what they are reading. Some of the books I have examined contain graphic descriptions not even suitable for adults.

Reflecting on the education that took place in colonised regions of Asia, Africa, and Latin America leads one to recognise that "education" often meant teaching the so-called natives self-hate. It is not surprising that many older people in these regions—including Pakistan—hold disturbing views about their own history; these views are the result of the colonial education they received. These very people then migrate to America, Canada, New Zealand, or Australia—and their children grow up without a high opinion of their native country.

Let us consider how we were made to feel negative about our own languages, or even how we came to believe that our languages were sources of division among us. Can you see how absurd it is to think that what is ours is the enemy, and what is not ours is our friend? That what is ours divides us, and what is foreign unites us?

It is **absurd**.

In all colonial situations, language is only one factor in the process of colonisation. The coloniser, in every context, suppresses the language of the colonised and elevates his own. This has been true throughout the subcontinent, across all African nations, and even in European countries such as Ireland.

In his work A View of the Present State of Irelande (1596), Spenser discussed future plans to establish control over Ireland. He warned of the dangers of allowing the education of children in the Irish language:

"So that the speech being Irish, the heart must needs be Irish; for out of the abundance of the heart, the tongue speaketh."

In this book there is a conversation between a visiting English lord from London and an English settler in Ireland. They discuss why they have been unable to establish full control over the Irish people—and how they

might succeed. They identify two strategies:
- **Destroy the naming system**—the way people name themselves;
- **Destroy the language.**

If they could suppress the Irish language and naming system, the people would soon forget who they were.

The same practice was applied in the Indian subcontinent and among the enslaved Afghan people—a project the colonisers referred to as "breaking them down" or "seasoning their language."

When Japan conquered Korea, the first thing it did was to ban Korean names and ban the Korean language. Why? Because to colonise a people, you must colonise their minds, their history, and the knowledge carried by their language. These are what give a people their sense of being a nation.

By erasing all this, colonisers alienated people from their own communities. Mentally, they were made to attach themselves to the conqueror's language and, consequently, to the conqueror's history, culture, and worldview. If you know all the languages of the world but do not know your mother tongue, then you possess only a servant's ligament. But if you know your mother tongue and then add the languages of the world to it, that is empowerment.

So the real choice is between:
- empowerment, and
- self-alienation.

When our forefathers realised their languages were being suppressed, they resisted by retaining the rhythms of Indian speech and adding them to other sounds, creating new languages that would carry meaning for them. Embedded within these languages were their culture, their philosophy of life, and their past—rich with the global influence of centuries. A language can give a people a sense of who they are.

As the poet said,

"Teach me to be me—the only way of teaching me to be me is through my relationship with my language."

Thus, Native Literature and Language must be at the centre, and from that centre one can radiate outward to other literatures. Every person in Pakistan has a right to his mother tongue or to the language of his culture. It does not matter if that language is spoken by only five people—those five have a right to their language and to the intellectual production of ideas within it.

That language can then relate to other languages through translation or by adding other languages to what one already possesses.

The problem in Pakistan—and in former colonies generally—is that the entire intellectual community operates through the English language, and the entire intellectual production of ideas is in a foreign language, while the majority of Pakistanis speak Pakistani languages. The Pakistani languages exist, but the language of power is English.

So the education that we look up to comes from Europe or America. Yet there is a fundamental unfairness embedded in the structure of American public education. Because of property taxes, all public education is not equal—it should be, but it is not. And I think it is important to acknowledge this, because only then can we question America's claim of having a system that is purely meritocratic.

From observing my friend's experiences, I came to understand that in America, race often becomes class. They see a brown child, and they cannot see anything beyond his brownness. There is often an automatic assumption that he must have come from an economically and educationally deprived background. But both of his parents—Pakistani immigrants—are doctors. This made me think about how many black and brown children, how many poor children of any race, are seen only in terms of their need, and thus grow up with their dignity eroded because they were not seen as full human beings, but merely as people "in need."

These doctor-parents have children who, I think it is fair to say, are not meek or mild-mannered. What the teacher said about their son—that he was "so rough"—is one way of describing him. But there is another way of seeing him: he is assertive and confident.

I am not suggesting that we excuse bad behaviour—bad behaviour should never be excused. And I must make a small confession: in American schools, there is a certain informality between instructor and student that I am not very fond of, because I think it sometimes blurs necessary boundaries and enables bad behaviour. But I am a Pakistani who belongs to a very strict school system.

The point I want to make about bad behaviour is this: When we sanction behaviour, we must be aware that sometimes we are not sanctioning the behaviour itself, but the **body exhibiting that behaviour.**

Chimamanda Ngozi Adichie, an African American writer, gives a powerful example. A black child was playing with a white child. The mother of the black child walked into the science room with the teacher. The teacher looked at the white child and said:

"Oh, that's so good—you're going to be a scientist!"

Then she looked at the black child and said:
"Oh, that's so good—you're going to be a mechanic."

The mother became very upset and confronted the teacher, who in turn became defensive and insisted she had not meant anything bad.

Yet something had clearly gone wrong.

Listening to the story, I imagined the two women inhabiting **two separate walls** that did not intersect. How do we bridge those walls? We must bridge them if public education is to succeed.

Perhaps if the teacher had understood the context of the child...
—his history as a black boy in a country that has systematically broken the dreams of black people,
—and also understood the stereotypes held by non-black people about black people,
...she might have chosen her words differently.

It takes a willingness to be uncomfortable.
It takes courage.
It is not easy.

But it is necessary if we want to mould a generation that will be better—and do better—than we have. We must broaden and widen our conception of how things are, and how things ought to be.

In all the colonised world, you will hear someone say:
"The teacher wasn't a good fit at my child's school."

Sometimes the reasoning is as superficial as this:
"The teacher had an inner-city accent."

He spoke English perfectly; his grammar was correct.

But because of his accent, he was deemed "not a good fit." We had a professor at the university with a heavy inner-city accent. He was perhaps the best teacher we had. Yet he was looked down upon by colleagues.

How do we define a "good fit"?

What determines it?

And would children not benefit from hearing someone who speaks differently?

His accent itself was a consequence of educational differences. Public education has a moral and civic duty to address such differences.

The purpose of education is **not** to maximise profit.
It is to **maximise human potential**.

Human potential is beautiful—gloriously messy, rudimentary, and impossible to contain within a single solution. There are many possible solutions.

Of course, English is spoken the world over, but in most countries it is merely a language of communication. In our country, however, it has become a carrier of culture. Culture embodies the moral, ethical, and aesthetic values through which people come to view themselves and their place in the universe. Values are the foundation of a people's identity—their sense of particularity as members of the human race.

All of this is carried by language.

Language, as culture, is the collective memory bank of a people's historical experience. But the most significant area of domination under colonialism has been the mental universe of the colonised—the control, through culture, of how people perceive themselves and their relationship with the world. To control a people's culture is to control their tools of self-definition in relation to others.

The point of education is not to maximize profit — it is to maximize human potential.

CHAPTER 8

Responsibility of Hiring

Teaching Is a Practice, Not a Perfection

Get off the Beaten Path. All jobs now require skills.

No school system is better than the caliber of its teachers. Although many elements must come together to create a successful school system, the people who directly influence students must be selected with great care. In fact, decisions concerning the selection of teachers are among the most crucial any principal must make.

Similarly, decisions about whether or not to retain teachers from year to year—particularly when these decisions involve tenure—form a vital part of a principal's role. A principal must have a sound, comprehensive system of teacher evaluation that includes teachers with tenure, part-time teachers, and those who are being considered for replacement because they have become ineffective or stagnant. No principal who takes his role seriously can leave this part of the job to chance.

Teacher's Evaluation

When we think of teacher evaluation, we too often view it narrowly in the context of hire-and-fire decisions. Although such decisions are important, evaluation should also serve an equally important purpose: providing a springboard for improvement.

We must instil in our teachers a spirit of change—one that compels them continually to ask:

- Whom am I reaching?
- Whom am I failing to reach?
- What am I doing that is successful?
- Where do I need improvement?

We need both kinds of evaluation:
1. Evaluation that guides decisions regarding employment status.
2. Evaluation that promotes professional growth and improvement.

Neither can be left to chance.

Let us first consider the more traditional concept of evaluation—evaluation for hire-and-fire purposes. Until very recently, decisions about who was a "good" teacher were based primarily on classroom discipline. I even heard of a headmaster who told new teachers that one way to judge their effectiveness was to look at the classroom floor: if it was littered with paper wads, then the teacher had not been effective that day, and the students had not been sufficiently inspired to behave responsibly.

The effect was predictable. Teachers simply made sure the paper wads were picked up before the janitor arrived to sweep at the end of the day. In essence, the janitor ended up evaluating the teachers. As a way of making the janitor's work easier, this technique was effective. As a method of evaluating teaching—self-evaluation or otherwise—it was not.

Other headmasters judged teachers by the number of boys sent to the office. In many cases, these superficial criteria were the only basis available for evaluation, because the headmaster seldom entered classrooms while lessons were in progress.

However sincere such efforts may have been, they were wholly inadequate. The result was predictable: if a teacher survived the probationary period, maintained reasonable classroom order, got along with colleagues, and did not "make waves," he could be almost certain he would receive tenure. In most cases, that was the last evaluation he ever saw.

This kind of staff evaluation can no longer suffice. If our schools are to meet the expectations placed upon them, they must have top-quality professionals performing to the best of their abilities. Neither outcome is possible without strong, meaningful evaluation from the principal.

The following criteria must be included:
- **Knowledge** of subject matter or area of expertise
- **Understanding of, and ability to relate to, students**
- **Skill and techniques of teaching**
- **Ability to maintain a classroom climate conducive to learning**
- **Ability to work as part of the school team**
- **Ability to relate well to parents and community members,** serving as a positive representative of the school

Personal characteristics that directly influence the

fulfilment of their professional role

Time and energy should not be wasted on irrelevant battles over minor personal traits. However, promptness, dependability, and acceptance of responsibility are essential elements of success in virtually every school situation.

Fortunately, this type of superficial supervision was rejected in most places years ago. More recently, principals have at least given lip service to the need to enter classrooms and conduct personal observations. However, in far too many cases, principals still do not know what to look for once they enter a classroom.

When principals observe often enough to understand the context of a lesson, their observations frequently focus on:

- room temperature,
- displays on the bulletin board,
- classroom decorations,
- or similar peripheral details.

These observations fall far short of their intended purpose.

Principals tasked with evaluating teaching effectiveness often concentrate on surface-level elements rather than on instructional quality.

For example, classroom observations often highlight:

- **Room aesthetics** (decorations, organisation)
- **Peripheral details** (lighting, temperature)
- **Displayed student work** (projects, posters)

But these overlook essential dynamics of teaching and learning, such as:

- **Teacher-student interactions and dialogue**
- **Instructional strategies and differentiation**
- **Assessment and feedback quality**
- **Student critical thinking and problem-solving**

Effective classroom observations should prioritise:
- Teaching practices that promote deep learning
- Student-centred instruction and authentic engagement
- Ongoing assessment and meaningful feedback loops
- Teacher reflection and continuous improvement

By embracing these principles, educators can transform classroom observation and feedback into powerful tools for professional growth and improved student outcomes.

Effective classroom observations and feedback are crucial for:
1. Enhancing teaching practices
2. Fostering collaborative staff cultures
3. Promoting student-centred learning
4. Developing teacher resilience
5. Improving student outcomes

After Hiring Teachers

A severe teacher shortage exists in our schools, and we have tens of thousands of teachers with sub-standard credentials. Principals must take all these individuals and mould them into an effective team—a team with a shared philosophy, clear goals, and purpose. The result, naturally, will include extreme highs and lows, with inconsistency being the order of the day.

A principal must begin by earning the respect of the staff, and this can only develop if the principal is consistent in his dealings with teachers. Teachers are told not to play favourites with students, and the same rule applies to principals: consistency and fair play must characterise the principal's relationship with staff.

There is no better way to energise teachers and uplift staff morale than by cultivating a school climate in which teachers feel safe, valued, and comfortable in their roles. This does not imply a lack of standards, an abdication of administrative responsibility, or an absence of supervision.

Being consistent in action, not over-reacting on behalf of parents, arranging reasonable in-service training opportunities, freeing teachers to teach, and involving them in decision-making—all of these are vital in developing and maintaining staff morale and a highly effective team.

An effective staff is one that:
- encourages students to challenge textbooks and teachers with thoughtful questions;
- accepts individual differences and idiosyncrasies;
- believes in freedom of thought and action;
- is committed to providing equal educational opportunities to every student.

Attempts to force teachers into a rigid mould or suppress their creativity are both wasteful and dangerous. Exceptional teachers will not tolerate such stifling. They will accept necessary organisation and respect strong leadership, but that organisation and leadership must be perceived as supportive, helping them accomplish their tasks—not as unnecessary restraints.

Effective classroom observations and feedback are transformative tools that foster teacher growth, student success, and overall school improvement. By prioritising instructional quality, using structured feedback models, and cultivating collaborative cultures, educators can create environments where teachers thrive and students excel.

Implementing these best practices requires:
- commitment,
- openness,
- and a willingness to adapt.

As educators, we must recognise the power of:
- constructive feedback,
- peer support, and
- ongoing professional development.

By embracing these principles, we can successfully bridge the gap between observation and improvement, ultimately enhancing the teaching-learning experience and shaping the future of education.

The Strength of a School Begins with the Strength of Its Teachers.

CHAPTER 9

Last Twenty-Nine Days

In those final nights, I learned the true weight of manhood.

The attack that took his life occurred when he was eighty-five years of age and resulted, ultimately, in the breakup of the family circle. For many years after his death, I could not pass Ganga Ram Hospital without noticing one particular window. It stood out from the rest —hallowed, because it represented the room where he had suffered so much. The details of those tragic days and nights remain in my memory, unchanged by the passage of time.

It was early morning when I saw him come out of the washroom, unsteady in his steps. I immediately realised something was wrong. He had his waistband in his hand. I helped him to his bed, tied the waistband, and asked him to rest. I called the doctor—the Medical Superintendent of Sir Ganga Ram Hospital, husband of our Lady Doctor in Junior School, and also my evening tennis partner. He arrived promptly within twenty minutes. After examining my father thoroughly, he told me to admit him to the hospital. He telephoned the hospital and arranged a bed.

By this time, the paralytic attack had become more severe, and my father slipped into a coma. He was shifted to the hospital within the hour. Thankfully, a team of doctors was ready for his assessment. The news was not encouraging. I was told to brace myself for the final call.

From then on, I endured twenty-nine days and twenty-nine nights practically without sleep—listening to him struggle for breath, listening to the sounds that seemed like the approach of death. My father lay in a deep coma. His heavy breathing echoed up and down the corridor.

On the third day, my father-in-law arrived to relieve my agony. Before that, my friends and I had walked the halls of that old hospital for hours, listening to the ceaseless struggle, which was now becoming fainter and fainter. Several times the nurse had called us in, and we had said our last good-bye—gone through the anguish of letting him go—only to have his heart rally again, and the endless vigil begin all over.

Finally, we moved into an adjoining room—not prepared for sleep, but some of us slumped across beds and chairs—falling into the sleep of utter exhaustion.
At five minutes to four o'clock, the nurse entered and awakened me. I started upright.

"Is he gone?" I asked.

"No," she said, "but if you want to see your dad one more time while he is still alive, you had better come now."

I quickly stood beside him. I smoothed back the hair from his forehead and laid my hand on his old, wrinkled hand—so very much like my own. I felt the fever that precedes death: 105 degrees.
While I was standing there, a change came over me. Instead of being a grown man (I was thirty-five at the time), I suddenly became a little boy again. They say this often happens to adults who witness the death of a

parent.

I imagined myself on the train nearing Lahore Railway Station, watching it move around the curve. My heart swelled with pride. I turned to a friend standing next to me and said:

"You see that man—with a smile on his face, that special smile? He looks like a different man. **That man is my dad!**"

The train stopped, and I jumped out to meet him. I had returned from the boarding house after about six months. He stoically patted me and asked for my luggage. He was a man who did not show his emotions—a man of few words—but he was a man of many kind actions.

As Shakespeare said:

**He hath heard that men of
few words are the best men**

It all came back. I patted his hand and said, "Good-bye, Dad," as he was sinking fast now.

I have never forgotten how hard you worked to send your children through college—how you wore those uniforms until they were slick.

My father-in-law had come in the morning to relieve me from my night's vigil. Half an hour later, he returned home to announce the news of his death.

He said that at **three minutes to seven o'clock**, like a stately ship moving slowly out of time's harbour into eternity's sea, my father breathed his last.

The nurse motioned for us to leave and pulled the sheet over his face—a gesture that struck terror in my heart. I turned away, silently weeping, and left the room. His death was marked by quietness and dignity, just like the life he had lived. Thus came to an end the affairs of

Syed Maqbool Hasan, and the solidarity of the family, too, ended. The old home place was never the same again. The old spirit that we had known as children was gone forever!

Again, this illustration reveals a few of the specific characteristics that Syed Maqbool Hasan had that made him so powerful an influence on his family; it also tells us how his son felt about him. I happen to know some of the other details. He was one of the oak trees – a man of strength and integrity. Although not a staunch Muslim until shortly before his death, he lived by an internal standard that was singularly uncompromising. He did his job with dead honesty and did full justice to the uniform he wore. He was once travelling to Karachi when he became suspicious of a beggar. He grabbed him and asked him to open his bag, despite protests from fellow passengers; the bag turned out to be full of money. God had given him the power to foresee and read human character. He took with him a clean conscience to his grave.

There were other admirable traits, of course, and many of them were transmitted to me. He personified much of what I'm trying to convey in this examination of manhood. He passed those values down to me. If men today were as certain of their masculine identity as my father, there would be far fewer lost boys who search vainly for role models in WWF or in popular culture.

Then I remembered something my mother had often said:

"All deaths are awful, but there is one thing I want you to remember: **we have said good night down here, but one of these days we are going to say good morning up there."**

I believe she did say "good morning," too—eleven years later.

His death was marked by quietness and dignity, just as his life had been. Thus came to an end the affairs of Syed Maqbool Hasan, and thus ended, too, the solidarity of our family. The old home was never the same again. The spirit we had known as children was gone forever.

Again, this illustration reveals only a few of the specific characteristics that made Syed Maqbool Hasan such a powerful influence within his family; yet it does tell us how his son felt about him. I happen to know some of the other details.

He was one of the oak trees—a man of strength and integrity. Although not a staunch Muslim until shortly before his death, he lived by an internal standard that was singularly uncompromising. He did his job with absolute honesty and did full justice to the uniform he wore.

Once, while travelling to Karachi, he became suspicious of a beggar. He detained him and demanded that he open his bag, despite protests from fellow passengers. The bag turned out to be full of money. God had given him the ability to foresee and read human character. He took a clean conscience to his grave.

There were other admirable traits, of course, many of which he passed on to me. He embodied much of what I am trying to convey in this examination of manhood. He modelled those values and transmitted them to me. If men today were as certain of their masculine identity as my father was, there would be far fewer lost boys searching vainly for role models in WWF or in popular culture.

Here are some important intellectual and moral distinctions that I derived from his life, and which I would advise young people to internalise:
- distinguishing needs from wants
- recognising real grown-up life versus life depicted on TV and in films

- understanding heroes versus mere "celebrities" and entertainers
- discerning courage from cowardice
- professionalism from careless sloppiness
- courtesy and good manners from boorishness
- integrity from disregard for truth and keeping one's word
- love for family and friends from selfish individualism

My purpose in sharing this reflection has been to urge young fathers to provide the modelling on which their sons can build their masculine identities. As you carry out the traditional roles I have described—or some version of them—your sons will observe who you are, and they will learn to serve in a similar way when they grow up.

That is why any advice to fathers about raising boys must begin with an examination of their own demeanour and character. Today, when the culture is in a tug-of-war with families for the hearts and minds of our children, we cannot afford to be casual about their care and training.

Where the ache of memory becomes the beginning of understanding.

CHAPTER 10

Masculinity

Frailty thy name is 'man'...As flies are to wanton boys are we to 'women'.

In continuation of last 29 days, let's look a little more closely at what it means to be a male. To me, it almost seems that maleness died with the end of my father's generation. It was the last generation that had everything under control. When I was a child, parents did not need to depend as much on communication and emotional closeness to keep their children in line. They could control and protect them, more or less, through the imposition of rules and the isolation created by their circumstances. Just a threat from my mother that we would be reported to our father was enough to keep us from going off the deep end.

The great advantage was that our older generation understood the system. They had a million rules. There were regulations and prohibitions for almost every imaginable situation. Coming from a very orthodox family, we were required to return home before dark. We were not allowed to use even mild slang. I remember being reprimanded for combing my hair in front of my mother's neighbourly friend. Our females were not allowed to appear in front of male cousins. Our girls were not allowed to laugh loudly, nor raise their voices—it was not considered decent.

considered decent.

The word *yaar*, now used so casually by both girls and boys, was then considered profane; we could not dare utter such a word. We did not dare say anything that even vaguely resembled profanity, even if it was nonsensical. Newly-weds were not allowed to hold hands; indeed, they were not allowed to sit on the same bed or sofa in front of their elders.

In those days, parental authority typically stood as a great shield against what was known as "the world." Anything considered unwholesome or immoral was kept firmly outside the walls of the home.

Fortunately, the surrounding community supported parents. It was structured to keep children on the straight and narrow path. Censorship prevented films from going too far. Schools maintained strict discipline; infractions were reported to parents. Cigarettes were not sold to minors. Motorcycles and cars were kept away from underage children. Illicit drugs were unheard of. Even adults outside the family saw it as their civic duty to help protect children from anything harmful—whether physical, emotional, or spiritual. Most of these neighbours were acquainted with the children's parents, which made it easier for them to intervene. This support system was generally effective.

Alas, that protective wall is gone. Harmful images and ideas slide under the front door and slither directly into bedrooms through electronic media. As the world has become more sexualised and more violent, there are now far too many opportunities for children to get into trouble. Furthermore, innumerable "voices" are out there enticing them to do what is wrong.

Parental authority is undermined at every turn. For example, when parents today decide not to allow their boys to see a bad movie, their instructions are likely to be disobeyed. The children might watch the film at a friend's house or on video when the parents are at work. And these days, adults seem to work longer and longer hours. That introduces one of the greatest points of danger: it is almost impossible for mothers and fathers to screen out harmful aspects of the culture when they are rarely at home in the afternoons. An unsupervised child can get into more mischief in a single day than his parents can undo in a year.

Maleness – Subject to Scorn

Today, everything associated with maleness is subjected to scorn. Men who cling to traditional roles and conservative attitudes are labelled "too macho." If they courteously open doors for ladies or offer their seats on a bus, as their fathers once did, they are branded "male chauvinist pigs." Women present themselves as victims who are "not gonna take it anymore," and men are cast as heartless oppressors who have allegedly abused and exploited womankind for centuries. Divorce has skyrocketed, as increasing numbers of women simply pack up and leave their husbands and children. Anger has become the watchword on TV talk shows and sitcoms.

The trap of masculinity—that is the way feminists describe maleness. A centrepiece of this hostility is the ongoing effort to convince society that "men are fools." According to this narrative, the majority of males are immature, impulsive, selfish, weak, and not very bright. The "stupid guy," as I will call him, quickly disgraces himself on screen. Hundreds of such advertisements appear on television today. Watch for them.

We must ask ourselves why there are so many of these "stupid guy" ads. The answer must be that they are effective—they increase sales of the products they promote. Advertising agencies conduct exhaustive market research before committing millions of corporate dollars to campaigns like these.

So what is happening here? Is it possible that men—especially tea-makers, sports-car enthusiasts, or those washing clothes or dishes, or flaunting wealth to trap a girl into marriage—actually like being depicted as dumb, horny, fat, nerdy, and unattractive? Apparently they do. We must also assume that men are not offended by the thousands of jokes made at their expense. But why?

Women would never tolerate such derision. You will notice that the polarity in these "stupid guy" ads is never reversed. Not in a million years would you see a corpulent, unattractive woman lusting after a handsome man who looks upon her with disdain as she behaves ridiculously. Men, however, do not seem to notice that they are the butt of the joke. Perhaps they (we) have been desensitised after years of such bashing.

This attitude has seeped into the Pakistani diaspora as well. Pakistani boys, not only overawed by living in a foreign land, willingly become obedient servants to their wives. I know of an example: a boy was literally picked from one of the most backward areas of Lahore to marry an American national. Within a year, he gained confidence along with a job and began to reveal his true character. He went on a world tour with his friends, never once taking his wife. Even now, it is common for boys from Pakistan to be sent for "ruksati" to America. Such boys are not serious about their careers; all they seek is a girl who does not wish to return home, so that they can command from a broad like "master's voice."

These lazy slobs—good for nothing—tarnish the image of those who remain in Pakistan, living voluntarily as men, providers. Such males are typically portrayed in Pakistani dramas and stories. In washing powder ads, icons like Wasim Akram appear cheerfully performing domestic chores. Frailty, thy name is man. As flies are to wanton boys, so are men to women.

In another advertisement, a man makes tea for a woman merely to earn the chance to watch a cricket match. In yet another, a prospective bride's condition for marriage is that the boy must know how to make tea.

Titanic

In the remake of the great ship Titanic, there were many accounts of masculine heroism as the vessel went down. Unfortunately, James Cameron, the director, chose to ignore them. Instead, he depicted the doomed men as cowardly and panic-stricken. In his version, hundreds of male passengers were kept out of the lifeboats at gunpoint. One man was shown sneaking past women and children and grabbing a precious seat.

History confirms that **few men behaved dishonourably,** but most did not. Only **325** men survived the sinking, and some of them were stewards assigned to take charge of the lifeboats. The beautiful young heroine, Rose, was a feisty girl who chose to go down with the ship. Her fiancé, Cal, was a despicable character who tried to bribe a steward for access to a lifeboat. When rebuffed, he grabbed a child and jumped aboard.

There can be no doubt that Cameron wanted viewers to believe that most male passengers would have stormed past women and children given the opportunity.

Suzanne Fields wrote:

"**If the Titanic were to go down today, there would be no 'women and children first.'**
A male coward wouldn't have to wear a dress to get into the lifeboats. Some of the women would help him aboard."

Despite the remarkable quality of Titanic and its special effects, the portrayal of men was characteristic of today's film industry. Rarely is an opportunity missed to depict males as self-serving, dishonest, misogynistic, or otherwise disrespectful. That is simply the way the game is played today.

In reality, the doomed men disappeared into the icy waters of the Atlantic so that their loved ones might survive to see another day. That is why the Titanic is still called the "**Ship of Widows.**"

These same trends have been observed in business settings, contributing to the feminisation of the workplace. When I began my career, there was only one female teaching Chemistry in the senior school. But over time, the number of women increased to 50 percent, then 75 percent. In middle school, they were already 25 percent, while in junior school there was only one male.
The female staff had been quiet and dignified. Suddenly, with the rise of the women's empowerment movement, they became more assertive—even aggressive. In the latter half of my career, I joined Pakistan's largest school chain. During my introduction to the school heads—who were all women—I, being the only male, jokingly introduced myself as "Mr Naila Hussain" to match the feminist inclination of the institution.

At one school, I had to give a presentation to an audience of two hundred ladies. I spotted four men sitting sheepishly at the back. I called them to the front, but they were too shy to comply. From there, I went to three more campuses, all dominated by women, before I was finally called back to my original institution—which had also become overwhelmingly female.

I realised that a man's career could be ruined by even the slightest implication, valid or invalid, that he had mistreated a female employee. The mere possibility of being accused of harassment has intimidated men—even when disciplinary action is needed or when disagreements arise between male supervisors and female subordinates. Many men in such situations are afraid to exercise necessary leadership if it risks displeasing or angering a woman. It feels safer to "**wimp out.**"

The best managers and leaders in the past were "take-charge" men—assertive and self-assured. Today, potential leaders are uncertain of how to operate, because it has become politically incorrect to be "macho" or traditionally masculine. It is time for men to act like men: respectful, thoughtful, and gentlemanly toward the women they love, yet confident, strong, and steady in their manner. Some have wimped out entirely, behaving like whipped puppies.

A balanced masculinity—anchored in dignity, responsibility, and quiet strength—remains essential. When men carry themselves with honour, both the family and society stand steadier.

"When strength is redefined, the measure of a man becomes the measure of a society."

CHAPTER 11

The Feminist Reversal: Redefining Gender Through Media

A Case Study in Hollywood's Gender Narrative

It is part of the feminist agenda to show women as powerful, courageous and indomitable, while men are weak, emotional and easily manipulated. The entertainment industry, which seems determined to unravel us, works hand in glove with feminists and homosexual activists to bring us into that brave new world. Its presentation of male and female role models is almost always perverted or warped in one way or another. Only recently, Joe Biden acknowledged that he had been struggling to come out and tell the truth, for he too deserved to live an honest life. He confessed he was gay.

A point can be illustrated by referring to the blockbuster movie Runaway Bride, released in 1999. It was one of the most popular films of the year. I would like to describe the storyline in detail because this film was classic feminist propaganda, but few viewers I have spoken to even noticed what the message of the movie truly was. It offered a blatant dramatization of the "new emasculated man" and the "new masculinised woman." The storyline was a ninety-minute celebration of sex-role reversals that contradicted convention at every turn.

It opened with the female star, Julia Roberts, racing through the trees on horseback, her gorgeous hair flowing behind and her wedding dress billowing in the wind. She had just left her third fiancé standing bewildered at the altar. Most girls dream from early childhood of having a romantic wedding someday, whereas guys are usually the ones who have trouble committing. In this film, however, the men were patsies who panted after this elusive, boy-like creature.

From the beginning, the episodes of sexual confusion came at the viewer in a dizzying array. Julia was at times a mechanic, a plumber and an air-conditioning specialist who created clunky-looking lamps out of electrical junk. She was very aggressive and selfish, in a charming sort of way. She managed her family's hardware store, drove an old pickup truck, often wore combat boots, and easily carried a heavy backpack that her boyfriend had difficulty lifting. When frustrated, she pounded and kicked a punching bag with a vengeance, grimacing and sweating profusely. At one point, the soundtrack included snippets of the pop rendition "She's a Man Eater." We got the connection.

Julia exhibited what has become known as "the new androgyny," embodying both stereotypically masculine and feminine characteristics. She had clean, delicate hands, manicured fingernails, creamy skin and a beautiful body, yet she earned her living doing greasy work and fighting like a man. No opportunity was missed to tell us that Julia was a "man." And yet, she was a pretty and delicate little thing.

Now consider how the movie handled the image of

manhood. The male lead, played by Richard Gere, was a winsome but rather wimpish and bumbling guy. He was between jobs, having been belittled and fired by his boss — who happened to have been his ex-wife. Everything he did ended in failure. Gere's ineptitude as a man was pathetic, whereas Julia excelled in all things masculine. After Gere's engine stalled, the two of them walked home through a grassy field, where she calmly told him there were many snakes underfoot. Terrified, Richard began hopscotching through the weeds like a barefooted kid on a hot sidewalk. Julia laughed and strolled along unconcerned. Yes, she was one tough dude, no doubt about that.

Clearly, Runaway Bride had a political agenda, as does almost every contemporary movie. This is the usual fare in today's films. Male characters are often depicted as stereotypically weak, lost, confused and rather feminine. On the other hand, the new heroines are aggressive and calculating. They have adopted all those traits they once scorned in men. They lie, they spy, they cheat, they plot revenge, they treat sex casually and then they slither away.

One last comment: you have seen movies that pit a beautiful woman against a tough-looking man. She cold-cocks him with a single blow. One of the absolutes in culture is that a man is never justified in hitting a woman, and for good reason. Women are not as strong as men and must be protected from male brutality. But when girls are shown holding their own and knocking out men twice their size, it undermines the rationale for the prohibition on violence of any sort against females, whether in marriage or anywhere else. As usual, the messages given to us by the entertainment industry are often destructive or downright silly.

Role of a Father

If character training is a primary goal of parenting — and I believe it is — then the best way to instil it is through the demeanour and behaviour of a father. Your sons will imitate much of what you do. If you blow up regularly and insult your wife, your boys will treat their mother and other females disrespectfully. If you curse or smoke or fight with your co-workers, your boys will probably follow suit. If you are selfish or mean or angry, you will see those characteristics displayed in the next generation.

Fortunately, the converse is also true. If you are honest, trustworthy, caring, loving, self-disciplined and God-fearing, your boys will be influenced by those traits as they age. If you are deeply committed to God and live by godly principles, your children will probably follow in your footsteps. So much depends on what they observe in you, for better or worse.

Someone said, "I'd rather see a sermon than hear one." There is truth to this statement. Children may not remember what you say, but they are usually impacted for life by what you do. Good illustrations of traditional and godly masculinity are hard to come by, but there is one example directly from my life and I want to write about it. It is about my father, who died at the age of about eighty-five.

I was very young when we travelled to Karachi and gathered with my father's three nephews, each a year younger than the other, yet the respect they gave one another was unbelievable. I was fortunate to spend part of the three days we stayed there reminiscing about their childhood and early home life. I recorded the discussions in my mind and was privileged to retain them. What a rich heritage this provided, granting insight into my father's life and theirs.

There were boisterous laughs, no banging of hands, no ridicule, no sarcasm. They were great listeners; never did they interject in anyone's conversation. While the conversation was of interest to me, there was a common thread that was especially significant throughout the three days. It focused on the respect with which they conversed with each other. They spoke to each other with unmistakable awe. I could clearly see they were men of enormous character and strength. This was reflected in their children as well, who also emulated love for one another.

Much later in life, we cousins discussed our elders:

"They were towers of strength."

"They had a certain dignity about them," said another, with an appropriate gesture.

"We held them in awe," replied the third.

It is difficult to summarise the subtleties and complexities of their personalities, and we were unable to find the right words. Only when we began talking about specific remembrances did the personality of these patriarchs become apparent.

Let us look more closely at what constitutes "a good family man" in today's world. To put that in perspective, it might be helpful to examine four traditional roles that men have played at home.

The first is to serve as the family provider. It was considered the father's role historically "to serve as the leader of the clan." Dad was the final arbitrator on issues of substance. Admittedly, this "headship" role was sometimes abused by selfish men who treated their wives with disrespect and their children like chattel, but that was never the way the assignment was intended to function. The system generally worked well for thousands of years.

The next contribution made by a father is to serve as protector. He shielded his family members from the outside world and taught them how to cope with it successfully. It was his responsibility to see that the house was safe at night and that the children were home at a reasonable time. Each member of the family felt a little more secure because he was there.

Finally, the next contribution made by an effective dad — although many failed in this role — was his obligation to teach the fundamentals of their faith. He was the interpreter of the family's moral code and sacred rituals, and he made sure the children went to the mosque every Friday. Admittedly, not many men in years past performed each of these duties adequately. But there was a broad consensus in the culture that this was what they were supposed to do.

Surrendering of Father's Role

Unfortunately, each of these roles has been ridiculed and attacked by postmodernists and their allies in the media. As a result, many fathers have a poor concept of what they are supposed to do or how to get it done. Some of them have surrendered their authority at home and are either altogether uninvolved, or they are trying to nurture their children in ways that are more characteristic of mothers. They have been told they need to be more sensitive and to learn to express themselves — to be more like women — and women are supposed to be more like men. This role reversal is terribly confusing to boys.

The culture is bearing down on families everywhere and threatening the welfare of their children. It has placed parents in a very difficult position. They must either close their eyes and ignore the harmful influences that are swirling around their kids, or they must figure out how to defend them.

The parents have to develop relationships with their kids. With all the temptations buzzing around our children, simply saying "no" a thousand times creates a spirit of defiance. Building up relationships should begin early and include having fun as a family: laughing and joking, playing board games, throwing or kicking a ball, shooting baskets, playing Ping-Pong, talking at bedtime, and doing a thousand other things that tend to cement the generations together.

The tricky part is to establish those friendships while maintaining parental authority and respect. It can be done. It must be done.

Experts say that when grown-up children were asked what they remembered most fondly from their childhood — was it the vacations they took, or the trips to theme parks or the zoo? — they answered, "No." It was when Dad got on the floor and wrestled with them. That is the way children think. It is especially the way boys think. The most meaningful activities in the family are often those simple interactions that build lasting connections between generations.

How to Build Relationship

First Five Minutes

A great idea relevant to relationships makes a lot of sense. It is called "the first five minutes" and is based on a book that was published many years ago. Its thesis was that the first five minutes occurring between people sets the tone for everything that is to follow. For example, a public speaker is given very few moments to convince his audience that he truly has something worthwhile to say. If he is boring or stilted in the beginning, his listeners will turn him off like a light bulb, and he will never know why. And if he hopes to use humour during a speech, he had better say something funny very quickly, or they will not believe he can make them laugh. The opportunity of the moment is lost. Fortunately, whenever we begin a new interaction, we have a chance to reset the mood.

This simple principle relates to family members as well. The first five minutes of the morning also determine how a mother will interact with her children on that day. Snarls or complaints as the kids gather for breakfast will sour their relationship for hours. Greeting children after school with kind words and a tasty snack may be remembered for decades. And at the end of the day, when a man arrives home from work, the way she greets her husband — or does not greet her husband — will influence their interaction throughout the evening. A single criticism such as, "Not aloo gosht again!" will put their relationship on edge.

To summarise, a close-knit family is what keeps boys grounded when the world is urging them to break loose. In this day and age, you dare not become disconnected, especially when everything is on the line. Strong relationships, built through simple daily interactions, become the anchor that steadies children against the pressures surrounding them.

A society loses its balance when it rewrites the nature of those who sustain it.

CHAPTER 12

The Undermining of Masculinity

When men abandon their duties, society abandons them.

I have many examples where the boys find themselves in trouble simply because of the absence of caring fathers. Everything associated with maleness was subjected to scorn. Men who clung to traditional roles and conservative attitudes were said to be too "macho." If they courteously opened doors for ladies or gave their seats on subways, as their fathers had done, they were called "male chauvinist pigs." Women presented themselves as victims who were "not gonna take it anymore," and men were portrayed as heartless oppressors who had abused and exploited womankind for centuries. Divorce skyrocketed, as a surprising number of women simply packed up and left their husbands and children. Anger became the watchword on TV talk shows and sitcoms.

Although early feminists raised some valid concerns — such as equal pay for equal work and discrimination in the workplace — they went far beyond legitimate grievances and began to tear at the fabric of the family.

By the time the storm had blown itself out, the institution of marriage had been shaken to its foundations, and masculinity itself was left reeling. It has never fully recovered.

The "trap of masculinity" — that is how feminists describe maleness. A central feature of this hostility is the ongoing effort to convince society that "men are fools," claiming that the majority of males are immature, impulsive, selfish, weak, and not very bright.

Even when films are not openly hostile to men, they often undermine respect for masculinity in subtler ways.

The Nashville Tennessean published a story indicating that women today think men do not measure up. A majority of women believe they are just as smart as men, and many think they are smarter. This stands in sharp contrast to our grandparents' view that men "knew best."

Another reason for the growing disrespect for men stems from rapid changes in the workplace. In 1950, for example, only one working-age woman in ten held a full-time job. Today, two-thirds of women either work or are actively seeking employment. For the first time in history, a working wife is likely to earn a wage comparable to that of her husband. Even when she is unemployed, she does not necessarily need a man to survive.

This shift began unsettling male confidence as early as the Second World War. Factories built portable crèches for the children of the women working in munitions industries. Those women discovered something many had not known before: they could perform jobs previously done only by men. When the men returned from war, women saw little reason to resume the subordinate role of the housewife. It became increasingly obvious that they did not need a man in order to survive.

Of course, there were advantages in this development. It gave women more freedom and independence — but it also introduced new strains. Some married women began to feel superior when they saw the financial struggles faced by single women. This change in attitude marked the beginning of miseries for many men. Much of this occurred in Western society. And what of Pakistan? The situation is even more troubling.

I know of many men in the Pakistani diaspora — particularly those who are overawed by life in a foreign land — who become obedient servants to their wives. I know of an example: a boy was brought from one of the most backward areas of Lahore to marry an American national. Once he gained confidence and secured a job, his true character emerged. He and his friends travelled the world, never once taking his wife with them. Even now, it is common for boys from Pakistan to be taken for rukhsati to America. These boys are not serious about their careers. All they want is a girl; and if she has no intention of returning home, then, like the "master's voice," they can issue commands from abroad.

These lazy slobs — good for nothing — tarnish the image of Pakistani men who live responsibly at home as providers. This category of men frequently appears in Pakistani dramas and stories.

In a washing-powder advertisement, Wasim Akram is shown happily washing clothes, presenting himself as if it were his civic duty. Frailty, thy name is man. As flies are to wanton boys, so are men to women. In a tea advertisement, a man is shown making tea merely for his wife's approval and for the privilege of watching a cricket match. In yet another, a prospective bride declares that her condition for marriage is that the boy must know how to make tea.

Most of these boys featured in such advertisements have selective capabilities — good only for mundane tasks such as washing clothes or washing dishes. But if a girl wishes to marry, she will marry only a "unique boy." It is strange that the boy's worthiness in these stories often comes down to his ability to make tea.

This "taming of the male" appears to be the direction society is taking. And it is not just confined to dramas or advertisements; it is reflected in attitudes and behaviours at home, in schools, and in workplaces. The idea that a man must prove his worth by acting like a servant — while the woman evaluates him like a schoolmistress — signals a deeper erosion of respect for traditional male roles.

The best managers and leaders in the past were "take-charge" men. A few had authoritarian styles, but most were firm, decisive, and confident — the kind of men who could be trusted with responsibility. Today such men are typically perceived as "sexist pigs" or as intolerably opinionated. Many men have therefore become timid, unsure of themselves, and afraid to express their opinions, especially in the presence of women.

The shift in social expectations has created confusion for many young men who are unsure whether they should be strong and dependable or soft and compliant. Instead of being appreciated for qualities such as courage, steadfastness, and a sense of duty, men are now often judged by how well they conform to a sentimental model of sensitivity.

This climate has produced a generation of males who are increasingly disengaged, directionless, and unwilling to shoulder responsibility. At the same time, society complains that men are irresponsible — not recognising that it has discouraged the very traits that once enabled men to lead, protect, and provide.

Women, on the other hand, have become more assertive, demanding, and self-assured. They know what they want and expect men to accommodate their expectations. Many women today are outspoken and confident — qualities that are admirable in themselves — but they often fail to recognise that men, too, need appreciation, respect, and encouragement.

The imbalance is striking: women are rewarded for boldness, while men are criticised for the very same trait. A woman who speaks her mind is considered empowered; a man who does so is often labelled arrogant or overbearing. Over time, this has cultivated a culture in which men suppress their natural strengths, unsure of how to act without being accused of insensitivity or aggression.

This shift has caused men to withdraw into silence and uncertainty, losing the confidence that earlier generations viewed as essential to manhood. As women ascend socially and professionally — which is a positive development — many men struggle to find their place in a world that increasingly questions the value of their traditional roles.

Boys are confused about what it means to be a man. They receive mixed signals from society, from the media, and even from their own homes. They are told to be strong, yet gentle; bold, yet cautious; confident, yet submissive. They are warned not to be "too masculine," and yet they are criticised for being weak or indecisive. The contradiction is paralysing.

A boy needs a clear model of manhood in order to grow into a responsible adult. But when every traditional trait of masculinity is mocked, rejected, or labelled oppressive, he is left without guidance. He does not know whether to emulate the assertive men of the past or the overly compliant men of today. As a result, many boys retreat from responsibility and lose their sense of direction.

This confusion is not accidental — it is the cumulative

result of decades of cultural messaging that demeans fathers, ridicules husbands, and mocks male leadership. When a society repeatedly portrays men as incompetent, foolish, or morally inferior, it should not be surprised when young men start believing it.

Fathers, who should have been the anchors of stability, have either stepped back or been pushed aside. In many homes, the father has been reduced to a silent figure — present, yet powerless; alive, yet without authority. Once, the father was a source of protection, discipline, and guidance. Now he is often treated as unnecessary or even as an obstacle.

The absence of strong, dependable fathers has created emotional voids that no school, no government programme, and no entertainment media can fill. Boys need fathers to model responsibility, courage, and restraint. Girls need fathers to model respectability, honour, and the kind of love that teaches them what to expect from a future husband.

When the father's role is undermined, the entire family structure weakens. Mothers become overburdened, children become confused, and society pays the price. A fatherless generation is left trying to construct an idea of manhood from fragments — from celebrities, from flawed fictional characters, or from peers who themselves lack guidance. The results are evident all around us.

The erosion of fatherhood has contributed to the rise of irresponsible men — men who do not feel accountable for their actions, their families, or their communities. When a boy grows up without witnessing responsibility in action, he seldom develops it within himself. He does not understand commitment because he has never seen it consistently demonstrated.

Irresponsibility becomes a cycle. A boy who grows up without proper guidance often becomes a man who repeats the same pattern: avoiding obligations, neglecting duties, and expecting others — especially women — to compensate for his shortcomings. Society criticises such men, yet it fails to recognise that it helped shape them.

At the same time, women increasingly shoulder roles that traditionally belonged to men. They work, manage households, raise children, and make major decisions. Many do all of this with remarkable resilience. But this shift has also created resentment and exhaustion. When women are forced to play both roles, they lose respect for men who abandon theirs.

The tragedy is that both genders suffer. Men feel unnecessary; women feel unsupported. Families weaken, children struggle, and society loses the balance that once held it together.

The modern classroom often adds to boys' confusion. Schools tend to reward quiet compliance and verbal expression — qualities more natural to girls — while boys' energy and restlessness are frequently labelled as misbehaviour. Rather than guiding them, many teachers expect boys to behave like girls, leaving them believing something is wrong simply for being male. With fewer male teachers in early schooling, boys rarely see male authority or leadership modelled, and this deepens their uncertainty about manhood.

Sports once offered a healthy outlet for competition and physicality, but even these environments now discourage traditional expressions of strength. Boys are urged to be gentle, restrained, and overly sensitive, creating a tension they cannot resolve. They are criticised when they act like boys and criticised again when they do not.

The erosion of fatherhood, the absence of clear male role

models, and the cultural suspicion of masculinity have produced a generation of young men unsure of their identity. Women, meanwhile, take on increasing responsibilities and grow frustrated with men who appear passive or confused. Both genders suffer: women feel unsupported, and men feel unnecessary.

A society that mocks fathers, belittles husbands, and portrays men as foolish cannot expect boys to grow into confident, responsible men. When masculinity is treated as a problem rather than a strength, we lose the balance that once held families — and communities — together.

"When a society teaches men to be ashamed of their strength, it should not be surprised when weakness becomes its norm."

CHAPTER 13

Adult Authority: A Crisis of Leadership, Culture, and the Upbringing of the Young

When adults lose confidence, children lose direction.

Adult authority has undergone a quiet yet profound transformation, and its effects are felt unmistakably in the world of modern education and family life. Teachers often struggle to motivate their pupils—not because children today lack intelligence or curiosity, but because the fabric of adult leadership that once supported orderly learning has weakened. In the absence of steady authority, adults sometimes attempt to captivate children by turning lessons into entertainment. This shift reveals something deeper: uncertainty about how to guide, how to instruct, and how to lead with confidence. When adults hesitate, children sense vulnerability, and the structure they rely upon begins to fracture.

A generation of teachers and parents now stands at the front of classrooms and homes with a quiet fear of judgement. Many adults are cautious not to appear too strict, hesitant to correct, and anxious about losing such hesitation. They need clarity, direction, and emotional steadiness. When adults lose conviction, children instinctively lose trust, and without trust, true learning cannot take root.

Educational institutions increasingly extend early-learning principles far beyond their appropriate age range. Play is an essential component of childhood, yet when it overshadows discipline, perseverance, and intellectual rigour, it deprives children of the challenges necessary for growth. In many schools, competitiveness is discouraged altogether, as though losing a game were an emotional injury rather than one of life's most valuable teachers. A child who never learns to lose gracefully may grow into an adult who cannot cope with failure. The avoidance of disappointment does not protect children; it weakens them.

More and more, ordinary childhood emotions are reframed as clinical disorders. A child reluctant to attend school is labelled with school phobia. Natural nervousness before examinations is reconstructed as an anxiety syndrome. Everyday fears—once soothed with reassurance and firm guidance—are now medicalised. Although well intentioned, these practices hinder children from developing the emotional resilience required for adulthood. A childhood from which all challenge is removed produces adults overwhelmed by even modest responsibilities.

At home, boundaries have softened. Many parents are reluctant to confront their children, even when misbehaviour is evident. I recall a mother who refused to believe her son had stolen a pen, insisting he would never lie. Only when he confessed did she accept the truth. Her struggle illustrates a broader trend: correcting a child feels uncomfortable, so parents avoid it. Yet it is precisely in these moments—when truth collides with tenderness—that character is formed. Teaching a child to acknowledge mistakes, apologise sincerely, and accept consequences is an irreplaceable lesson.

Parents today often shoulder responsibilities their children should be learning. Simple skills such as cooking, cleaning, organising, and managing homework are sometimes taken over by adults who wish to ease their children's burdens. These actions, though tender in intention, limit a child's capacity to develop independence. When such children become adults, they often find themselves unprepared for the routines and pressures of daily life. Without boundaries and discipline, they grow up believing that the world will accommodate their wishes as freely as their homes once did.

The decline of respect for professional roles further compounds these difficulties. Teachers are now frequently referred to as facilitators, and classrooms are described as learning communities in which all participants occupy the same level. Academic rigour is sometimes replaced with broad-based skill activities that lack depth or direction. As the professional standing of educators diminishes, so does the respect they command from students. When students no longer regard their teachers as authoritative figures, learning suffers, and the foundational purpose of education begins to erode.

Children thrive on warmth, affection, and encouragement, but these alone are not enough. They also require firm boundaries, consistent discipline, and moral clarity. They need to know where safety lies, whom to trust, and who will guide them. A child must be able to rely upon the quiet strength of parents whose love includes the courage to say no. Discipline, when offered with tenderness, does not diminish a child; it strengthens him. It builds patience, fosters self-control, and nurtures respect.

Endless positivity, though pleasant, cannot take the place of thoughtful restraint. Protective caution teaches children to pause, to evaluate, and to avoid harm. It is this internal compass—shaped by firm yet gentle correction—that prevents reckless behaviour and shields young hearts from destructive paths. Many sacred teachings are framed in prohibitions not to restrict life but to preserve it. Through the boundaries we set, children learn the value of moral safety.

Parents may offer their children material comforts in abundance, but material gifts without a moral and spiritual grounding ring hollow. Children learn far more from observing the lives of their parents than from hearing their words. A parent's integrity, faith, patience, and compassion leave deeper imprints than any instruction. When adults falter in consistency, children inherit those same fractures in amplified form.

Raising a child resembles preparing a glider for flight. At first, the glider requires guidance, steadying hands, and careful control. But eventually the tow-rope must be released, and the glider must soar on its own. When adult authority weakens, we deprive the next generation of the security required to take flight. As the world around them grows more complex, children need stronger anchors than ever.

There was a time when neighbours offered counsel, teachers were honoured, and community values provided a stable backdrop for childhood. But with digital influences entering homes at all hours, and with cultural messages sometimes working against parental guidance, children navigate complexities too soon. Without confident adults to interpret these messages, they are left to make sense of the world alone.

Yet hope remains. By acknowledging these challenges, we begin the work of rebuilding the foundations of family, school, and community life. When adults embrace their roles with steadiness and courage, they become the anchors children instinctively seek. Authority reclaimed is not harsh or authoritarian; it is protective, compassionate, and wise.

Strength is renewed in a generation when adults accept their roles not with severity but with firmness; not with permissiveness but with balanced wisdom. The future will be shaped by those willing to stand steady, to speak truth with kindness, and to guide with compassion. In choosing this path, we offer children more than comfort—we offer them the confidence to dream, the courage to endure, and the strength to soar.

There is, however, an even deeper dimension to this crisis of authority—one that rests in the quiet habits of daily life. Children observe far more than we realise. They watch how adults speak to one another, how they resolve disagreements, how they treat time, how they respond to frustration, and how they cope with uncertainty. These small, invisible lessons shape their understanding of maturity. When adults rush, complain, compare, or grow impatient at the slightest inconvenience, children internalise the same fragility. But when adults model steadiness, thoughtfulness, and patience, children absorb these qualities just as effortlessly.

For many young people today, life is a constant rush of stimulus. Endless entertainment, instant gratification, and digital noise have created an atmosphere in which attention is fragmented and stillness feels foreign. Without adults who deliberately cultivate calmness, children seldom discover it on their own. A quiet home, a consistent routine, and a predictable rhythm once provided a kind of emotional scaffolding. In their absence, children may drift through life yearning for a sense of stability they never experienced.

Another part of the struggle lies in the way society glorifies self-expression while neglecting self-control.

Children are often encouraged to "speak their truth," "follow their feelings," and "prioritise themselves." While there is value in emotional honesty, the unbalanced elevation of personal feeling over personal responsibility creates confusion. Feelings, powerful as they are, cannot become the compass for life. The adults who guided earlier generations knew that the heart is best protected by discipline, humility, and awareness of consequences. When these values disappear, children find themselves overwhelmed by emotions they do not know how to regulate.

The most powerful lessons a child learns are rarely taught explicitly. They are absorbed in silence—watching a father wake for prayer when the world sleeps, observing a mother speak kindly even when tired, witnessing how adults restrain their anger or honour their commitments. These moments teach more than lectures ever could. In a world filled with loud messages, it is these quiet, consistent acts that shape a child's understanding of integrity.

Yet despite the challenges of modern life, children remain remarkably receptive to love that is both gentle and firm. They flourish when adults listen to them with sincerity, when their sorrows are taken seriously, and when their efforts—however small—are acknowledged. But they flourish equally when adults dare to set limits, to say "not yet," "not this," and "not in this house." This balance between affection and firmness is the essence of meaningful guidance. Without it, children may receive comfort, but they will lack character.

Children now grow up amid rapid change, yet their deepest needs remain the same: security, guidance, affection, faith, and the steady presence of adults who know who they are. When these needs are met, children rise with courage; when neglected, even small pressures feel overwhelming.

This is why the adult's role is sacred. Every act of patience, every boundary set with kindness, and every moment of moral clarity becomes a seed that outlives us. A child does not remember a parent's perfection, only their effort—the warmth, honesty, routines, and the feeling that home was safe. From these memories, their understanding of adulthood is formed.

If adults reclaim their role with calm conviction—not harshly nor indulgently—then the next generation will stand steadier than the last. Authority, gently restored, becomes a shelter of meaning, teaching children not merely to survive but to move through life with dignity and restraint.

Such children do not simply grow; they unfold.
And perhaps this is the truest hope: that in strengthening ourselves, we strengthen those who will outlive us. Each generation inherits both the wisdom and the wounds of the one before it. When we choose steadiness over haste and truth over convenience, we offer a better inheritance —one of clarity, balance, and moral courage.

No single chapter completes understanding. Life reveals itself in layers, and each reflection opens the way to another. If this book has encouraged its readers to pause, observe, and reconsider the foundations upon which we raise our children and shape our lives, then its purpose has only begun.

For there is more to explore, more to question, and more to understand.

The journey continues, and the next reflections await.

"Strength is renewed in a generation when the adults embrace their roles once more."

AFTERWORD

The Journey continues..........

In this first book, each essay ventures into seldom-explored thoughts—where words inspire rather than debate. Reflection is a soulful journey, not a destination. Every insight raises deeper questions; every truth found urges further discovery.

If this book has unsettled the comfort of convention, it has fulfilled its purpose. Truth isn't here to soothe; it's here to awaken. These pages begin a conversation that persists, not just in words, but through a gradual, thoughtful awakening of consciousness that our times desperately need.

The upcoming volumes won't repeat these ideas but will build upon them. They'll explore the silent effects of ideas nurtured here: how language shapes identity, how education fosters dependence, how authority stumbles without morality, and how faith alone unites a fragmented mind. Each volume will reflect a new phase of our shared rediscovery.

Let this be seen not as an end but as a promise—a commitment that the conversation will continue until reflection becomes a way of life. Seeking clarity isn't just about books; it's about a lifelong commitment to face truth with clear eyes.

May these reflections grow.
May they reach beyond these pages—into hearts that dare to think, question, and remember.

Sayed Amir Hussain
Lahore, Pakistan
November, 2025

ABOUT THE AUTHOR

Sayed Amir Hussain has dedicated over forty transformative years to the field of education, embracing roles such as teacher, mentor, school head, and guiding light for countless children and educators. His journey is a beacon of integrity, respect for each child's emotions, and a visionary belief in the boundless potential of education.

Throughout the decades, he has been a catalyst for change, shaping school cultures, enhancing teaching methods, and championing learning environments grounded in dignity, compassion, and honesty. His work stands as a testament to the power of experience, the clarity of insight, and unwavering moral strength—qualities that have earned him the enduring admiration of both teachers and students.

Even now, he continues to write and reflect, contributing to education with a passionate purpose: to honor children, empower teachers, and inspire a more humane and enlightened approach to schooling. His legacy is not only a career but a lifelong mission to ignite the spark of possibility in every mind he touches.

www.ingramcontent.com/pod-product-compliance
Lightning Source LLC
Chambersburg PA
CBHW020935090426
42736CB00010B/1142